Keto Chaffle

The Ultimate Cookbook with Easy Recipes which will teach you How to prepare Delicious Ketogenic Waffles for your Low Carb and Gluten .

COPYRIGHT

—

CONTENTS

COPYRIGHT 3

INTRODUCTION 10
   MIXED BERRY CHAFFLES 12
   PEANUT BUTTER AND JELLY CHAFFLES 14

SAVORY CHAFFLES 19
   CORNBREAD AND JALAPENOS 21
   BACON, EGG AND CHEESE CHAFFLE 28
   FANCY ROSEMARY AND GOAT CHEESE PANINI.......................31
   CARLIC BRAD CHAFFLE 34
   BAKED POTATO LOW CARB CHAFFLE......................................44

DESSERTS 46
   SUGAR COOKIE CHAFFLES 47
   CHOCOLATE CHIP COOKIE CHAFFLE 49
   GINGERBREAD 56
   BOSTOM CREAM PIE CHAFFLE 61
   BANANA NUT CHAFFLES 65
   CARROT CAKE CHAFFLE 72
   PECAN PIE CHAFFLE..87

A CHAFFLE BY ANY OTHER NAME...98

CONCLUSION 107

INTRODUCTION

Sugar, any of different common and artificial substances that give a sweet preference for nourishment and refreshments. Notwithstanding their improving force, they might be utilized for such procedures as nourishment safeguarding, aging (in blending and wine making), heating (where they add to surface, tenderization, and raising), and nourishment sautéing and caramelization. Regular sugars might be both nutritive and flavorable and in this manner well known both as nourishment and seasoning. Nonetheless, because normal sugar and other nutritive sugars, for example, nectar and corn syrup are related with health issues, (for example, weight and tooth rot) or are even a risk to life (for diabetics), there have been endeavors since the nineteenth century to create nonnutritive sugars that are not dependent upon digestion and contain practically zero caloric worth. Nonnutritive sugars, which might be either artificial (manufactured) or got from plants, incorporate such mixes as saccharin, aspartame, cyclamates, and thaumatin.

MIXED BERRY CHAFFLES

I am in this with this Easy Blueberry Chaffle Recipe! You can utilize new blueberries or you can utilize a blueberry extricate when they are out of season as well. We spread a layer of genuine margarine over our hot Blueberry Chaffle and afterward cleaned it with a touch of confectioners monkfruit. It was fabulous! The kiddos ate it up and requested more!

Simple Blueberry Chaffle Recipe

If you love chaffles as much as we do, I might want to by and by welcome you to our most current Facebook gathering: Keto Chaffle Recipes

This gathering is developing at record speed pace! We had almost 12000 individuals participate in just shy of about fourteen days! There are huge amounts of new recipes and tips being post every day! Come go along with us! We couldn't want anything more than to have you be a piece of our locale!

You can make this Easy Blueberry Chaffle Recipe early. They warm up pleasantly noticeable all around fryer or toaster stove in only a couple of moments! They will last around 4 to 5 days in the fridge as well.

You know what else? This Easy Blueberry Chaffle Recipe would likewise make a great blueberry cake as well. I'm as of now considering making it into a cake just by including a touch of icing. It's a superb method to remain on track with the keto diet without going over the edge on a festival.

We bought these adorable minimal individual size cake plates only for these pastry chaffles! Did you see the adorable Pumpkin Cake Chaffle Recipe we posted recently! It's gone insane viral and everybody is adoring that recipe.

Simple BLUEBERRY CHAFFLE RECIPE INGREDIENTS

1 egg
3 tablespoons almond flour
1 tablespoon cream cheddar
1/4 teaspoon heating powder
5 or 6 blueberries
1 teaspoon blueberry separate, discretionary

Simple BLUEBERRY CHAFFLE RECIPE INSTRUCTIONS
Preheat waffle producer.

In a little bowl, whip the egg.

Include the rest of the fixings.

Splash the waffle creator with nonstick cooking shower.

Separation blend down the middle.

Cook a large portion of the blend for around 3 to 4 minutes or until brilliant dark colored.

Top with these potential alternatives: dust with monkfruit, more blueberries, whipped cream, icing, or simply eat it plain.

PEANUT BUTTER AND JELLY CHAFFLES

If you have been needing a nutty spread chaffle, then you are going to LOVE this Peanut Butter Chaffle recipe. It is easy to make and has the ideal nutty spread flavor!

Nutty spread Chaffle

Something that is ordinarily a no go fit as a fiddle or structure when you are eating low carb is a nutty spread and jam sandwich. Bread is a no go and most jams are a no go. Thanya who is a marvelous aide here disclosed to me that she was missing nutty spread and jam sandwiches.

She disclosed to me that and afterward I began needing a nutty spread and jam sandwich. I avoided the enticement of making one and got the opportunity to work making an astounding nutty spread chaffle that would work superbly as a feature of a nutty spread and jam sandwich.

Just put a chaffle is a waffle made with egg and cheddar. Presently from the essential chaffle recipe you can make MANY different assortments of chaffles simply switching up the kind of cheddar that you use.

You can likewise switch up the flavors by adding different things to the essential chaffle recipe. There are truly unlimited potential outcomes when making keto chaffles.

What do you cook a chaffle in?

I cook my chaffles in the smaller than normal Dash Waffle producer because it is adorable, minor and makes the ideal size for me chaffles. If you need to utilize a normal estimated waffle producer you can.

The difference is that with a small waffle producer this recipe will make 2 chaffles, a standard estimated waffle creator it will make 1 keto chaffle. You can utilize both estimated waffle creators, I just truly love my smaller than usual one because it is so darn charming!

If you are new to making chaffles make certain to look at how to make a chaffle for the best keto chaffle recipe. This is the place all chaffles, including this Peanut spread Chocolate Chip chaffle recipe start.

What to Serve with a Peanut Butter Chaffle?
You can serve this chaffle a couple of different ways and have a tasty chaffle. You can top it with natively constructed keto whipped cream, confectioners' sugar or simply appreciate it independent from anyone else. Notwithstanding, my preferred method to appreciate it is as a nutty spread sandwich!

NUTTY SPREAD CHAFFLE

Keto Peanut Butter and Jelly Sandwich

I made my Keto Peanut Butter and Jelly sandwich utilizing sugar free grape jam. In any case, I wager this keto nutty spread and jam would taste astonishing with Sugar free Blackberry Jelly or Sugar free Strawberry jam.

To make a Keto Peanut Butter and Jelly cook your nutty spread chaffles. Then spread a layer of nutty spread on one and jam on the other. Close them up simply like you would a sandwich and appreciate!

Made with cinnamon chaffle bread and blueberry compote, this Peanut Butter and Jelly Sammich Chaffle is going to make you love being on the keto diet much more!

Made with cinnamon chaffle bread and blueberry compote, this Peanut Butter and Jelly Sammich Chaffle is going to make you love being on the keto diet significantly more!

Enormous on account of Cheryl W. from the Keto Chaffle Recipes Group for offering these astounding recipes to us!

Once in a while YOU JUST NEED A GOOD OLE PB&J Sammich!

Nutty spread and JELLY SAMMICH CHAFFLE INGREDIENTS

2 eggs

1/4 cup mozzarella

1 tsp cinnamon

1 T Swerve Confectioners

2 tsp coconut flour

1/8 tsp heating powder

1 tsp vanilla concentrate

BLUEBERRY COMPOTE INGREDIENTS

1 cup blueberries, washed

Pizzazz of 1/2 lemon

1 T lemon juice, crisply crushed

1 T Swerve Confectioners

1/8 tsp thickener

2 T water

BLUEBERRY COMPOTE INSTRUCTIONS

Add everything aside from thickener to little pot.

Heat to the point of boiling, diminish warmth and stew for 5-10 minutes until it begins to thicken.

Sprinkle with thickener and mix well.

Expel from warmth and let cool.

Store in fridge until prepared to utilize.

NUTTY SPREAD AND JELLY SAMMICH CHAFFLE RECIPE NUTRITION

Makes 4 Chaffles. Every Cinnamon Chaffle is 1.25 net carbs.

Compote is 1.6 net carbs/Tablespoon.

PB will rely upon what brand you pick and the amount you use.

The Keto Starter Guide is an astounding asset as you begin on your keto/low carb venture. This guide has all that you have to begin in 9 basic video exercises and furthermore incorporates exercise manuals with bit by bit directions for learners.

What's a full scale and for what reason do I check them?

How would I locate the best recipes?

What is ketosis and how would I get my body there?

What natural products are permitted on a ketogenic diet?

Will I get "Keto Flu" and what do I do about it?

SAVORY CHAFFLES

CORNBREAD AND JALAPENOS

This jalapeno cornbread recipe is unfathomably damp with bunches of fiery jalapeno peppers and cheddar. Incredible for these special seasons or a whenever side dish!

Lift your hand if you love jalapeño cornbread! You can't see me, however my hand is about contacting the roof at this moment. For me, there is nothing superior to a soggy, practically delicious bit of cornbread that is stuck brimming with cleaved jalapeno peppers and a touch of great melty cheddar.

The main individual I realize who adores cornbread more than I do is my wife, Patty. She is CRAZY for cornbread and needs it significantly more than I do. That is stating a great deal!

What's so GREAT about cornbread is its adaptability.

WHAT TO SERVE WITH JALAPENO CORNBREAD – IT'S SO VERSATILE!

Cornbread fits consummately as a straightforward side dish to such a large number of different dinners, from huge dishes of gumbo to bean stew to everything without exception BBQ. I can't envision BBQ pulled pork or BBQ ribs without my cornbread! You can likewise serve it as a dinner starter, a tad of jalapeno cornbread before the fundamental course is served.

One of my preferred approaches to serve it, however, is as treat. Have a go at showering a touch of nectar over a cut of jalapeno cornbread. Promised it will get one of your preferred sweets ever.

The main drawback to cornbread I've seen is that it very well may be dry. God help us! No one needs dry cornbread! I sure don't. There is a mystery, however, to making cornbread that is soggy and not dry. You'll see that mystery in the recipe, and more on that underneath.

Above all, we should discuss how we make this amazing jalapeno cornbread, will we?

Two cuts of Jalapeno Cornbread dribbling with nectar

Fixings NEEDED FOR JALAPENO CORNBREAD

1 cup entire milk

4 tablespoons liquefied spread

2 huge eggs

14.5 ounces creamed corn (1 can)

1 cup cornmeal

1 cup generally useful flour

3 tablespoons sugar

1 tablespoon salt

2 teaspoons preparing powder

1 teaspoon preparing pop

½ teaspoon dark pepper

1 cup cleaved jalapeno peppers + cut jalapenos for fixing

1 cup destroyed cheddar (or utilize a hot pepperjack for additional warmth)

The most effective method to MAKE JALAPENO CORNBREAD – THE RECIPE STEPS

Warmth your broiler to 375 degrees F (190 degrees C).

Whisk together the milk, softened spread, eggs and creamed corn together in a little bowl.

Join the cornmeal, flour, sugar, salt, preparing powder, heating pop, and dark pepper in a different bigger bowl.

Empty the wet fixings into the dry fixings and mix together.

Mix in the slashed jalapenos and destroyed cheddar.

Empty the player blend into a daintily oiled preparing dish and heat for 25-35 minutes, or until the cornbread sets and when a toothpick embedded in the middle confesses all.

Cool marginally, cut and serve.

Makes 9 bits of cornbread.

A cut of Jalapeno Cornbread on a plate, dribbling with nectar.

THE SECRET TO MOIST CORNBREAD

The mystery fixing to preparing damp cornbread is creamed corn. Creamed corn is produced using sweet corn and incorporates the smooth buildup from the corn cobs. The additional dampness moves to the cornbread to a for all intents and purposes fall flat confirmation recipe. If you don't need dry cornbread, get yourself a container of creamed corn. You'll express gratitude toward me for it.

RECIPE TIPS and NOTES

Make Double. This group makes 9 great estimated squares of clammy and feathery cornbread. You can without much of a stretch twofold or even triple the clump and heat it in discrete preparing dishes.

Spread it Out. If you utilize a more extensive skillet, you can make a similar clump of cornbread, however more slender, so the cuts are just a large portion of the size of mine. This will yield you about 18 bits of littler cornbread. This is a decent method to extend the recipe for bigger social events. Simply don't prepare it for very as long.

Additional Jalapenos. If you'e like it additional zesty, you can without much of a stretch incorporate more jalapeno peppers into your group.

Make it Cheesy. Cheddar is another fixings here that is anything but difficult to incorporate. I've utilize a cup for my recipe, however you can pretty effectively incorporate another 1/2 or more. Give it a go!

Jalapenos on Top. I like to add additional jalapeno cuts to the highest points of the hitter before preparing for an extra brightening touch. It looks incredible along these lines!

Sprinkle with Honey. One of my preferred approaches to present jalapeno cornbread is with a decent shower of sweet nectar. Such a brilliant flavor blend.

Additional Corn. If you like your cornbread with loads of corn, include a cup or 2 of additional corn portions. The recipe will cherish you for it!

Fixings

1 cup entire milk
4 tablespoons softened spread
2 enormous eggs
14.5 ounces creamed corn 1 can
1 cup cornmeal
1 cup universally handy flour
3 tablespoons sugar
1 tablespoon salt
2 teaspoons heating powder
1 teaspoon heating pop
½ teaspoon dark pepper
1 cup slashed jalapeno peppers + cut jalapenos for fixing
1 cup destroyed cheddar or utilize a zesty pepperjack for additional warmth

Directions

Warmth stove to 375 degrees F (190 degrees C).

Whisk together the milk, dissolved spread, eggs and creamed corn together in a little bowl.

In a bigger bowl, consolidate the cornmeal, flour, sugar, salt, preparing powder, heating pop, and dark pepper.

Empty the wet fixings into the dry fixings and mix together.

Mix in the hacked jalapenos and destroyed cheddar.

Empty the hitter blend into a daintily oiled preparing dish and heat for 25-35 minutes, or until the cornbread sets and an embedded toothpick turns out dry in the middle.

Cool somewhat, cut and serve.

A recipe for custom made cornbread with a lot of sweet corn and slashed jalapeno peppers, prepared right in the skillet. It's the ideal side dish.

Cornbread and stew peppers are best buds, particularly jalapeno peppers. I don't figure I can have cornbread any longer WITHOUT some scrumptious bean stew peppers heated in. We made this for a gathering and it vanished before long. The test with cornbread is to guarantee it doesn't get excessively dry.

It can undoubtedly dry out if you're not cautious, and no one needs cornbread that simply kind of thumps in your mouth. It should be soggy, practically like a cake. The keys here are joining the darker spread and brew. You'll get a lot of dampness in the subsequent cornbread. So great!

It's a magnificent side dish, however we've likewise served it as a tidbit and it generally goes quick, so you should make an additional cluster. You can utilize biscuit tins for this cornbread recipe, yet the skillet works out amazing for cornbread, and you can teach it a thing or two in the skillet.

It's a pleasant touch for when you're hoping to have an effect with your visitors. I like to serve this with some kind of jam or jam, similar to our custom made habanero jam or a decent jalapeno jam. Nectar is a pleasant expansion also.

PATTY'S PERSPECTIVE

If you're stressed over this being too zesty because of the jalapeno peppers, no need. This recipe isn't zesty, so you can don't hesitate to be liberal with them. More jalapenos is better! What's more, the sweetness from the corn is so delectable.

Fixings

1-1/2 cups cornmeal stone ground is ideal

1-1/2 cups flour
1 tablespoon salt
2 teaspoons preparing powder
½ teaspoon preparing pop
½ teaspoon ground dark pepper
½ cup destroyed cheddar
1 cup entire milk
12 ounces brew
3 huge eggs
1 stick unsalted spread
Corn from 1 huge fresh corn should yield around 1 cup
4-5 jalapeno peppers hacked

Directions

Warmth the stove to 375 degrees.

In a huge bowl, include cornmeal, flour, salt, heating powder, preparing pop and pepper. Blend. Include the cheddar and blend well.

In a different bowl, include milk, lager and eggs. Whisk it up pleasantly until smooth.

Include the wet fixings into the dry fixings and blend to shape your hitter.

Warmth an enormous cast iron dish to medium warmth and include margarine. Permit to soften and turn marginally darker, only a couple of moments.

Include corn and jalapeno peppers. Cook around 2 minutes, or until corn just starts to change shading. Cool marginally and blend everything into the player.

Empty the player once more into the cast iron dish and prepare for 25-35 minutes, or until it you can embed a toothpick into the inside and it hauls out dry.

Permit to cool. Cut and serve.

Gooey JALAPENO POPPER CORNBREAD MUFFINS

This cornbread recipe makes the ideal occasion side dish or hors d'oeuvre. Clammy cornbread biscuits loaded up with cream cheddar and bested with jalapeno pepper cuts. Watch them vanish.

Cornbread in the house! Raise your hand if you love cornbread? I unquestionably do, and when the Christmas season moves around, I will in general start contemplating a decent bunch of cornbread to serve. Cornbread is constantly well known and it tends to be filled in as either a side dish or a canapé, or both! Whichever you like.

They're likewise very basic to serve nearby your preferred bean stew recipes. We simply hosted a major neighborhood get-together and I was accountable for the cornbread, so I prepared this group and they vanished. These are somewhat different, be that as it may, than your average cornbread recipe. Why? Because these cornbread biscuits are...

Indeed!

These cornbread biscuits are loaded up with a dab of cream cheddar, then beat with a cut of jalapeno pepper, so each and every biscuit nibble experiences cream cheddar and eruption of jalapeno enhance.

They're sufficiently simple to make, which is constantly a reward for me. More or less, you'll combine the dry fixings, then mix in the wet fixings to shape your player. Spoon the hitter into your little biscuit tins, however, just fill them 3/4 full.

Next, spoon a little segment of cream cheddar over every one of the player filled tins. You extremely just need around 1/eighth of an ounce, however you could without much of a stretch fit more if you'd like, so be set up with additional cream cheddar, in the event of some unforeseen issue. Push the cream cheddar down into the player and go through a spoon to cover it with hitter.

At last, top every biscuit with a jalapeno pepper cut, as so.

Heat those children up! They're amazing!

I utilized small scale biscuit tins for this situation, and the recipe makes 48 little biscuits, yet you can without much of a stretch utilize bigger biscuit tins if you'd like. Simply make certain to modify your heating times to oblige.

As I referenced, these make and remarkable side dish, however I additionally prefer to serve them as tidbits. Extraordinary stuff!

Tell me how they show up for you. I trust you appreciate them.

BACON, EGG AND CHEESE CHAFFLE

We just got a smaller than expected waffle creator and it has become an immense hit in our home! We have utilized it around multiple times in the previous 3 days! We have been making Keto Chaffles which are fundamentally egg and cheddar and whatever else you need to blend in.

We have made treats, flame broiled cheddar sandwiches, Belgium waffles, and that's only the tip of the iceberg. My children even love utilizing it and are having some good times thinking of new things to make with it.

We are additionally attempting to eat less sugar and flour so making these bacon, egg, and cheddar chaffles have been ideal for the morning surge. Everyone takes about 2:30 minutes to make.

I don't care for the surface of fried eggs, however I love the delightful way these have somewhat fresh to them and are truly filling and brimming with season.

Recently I made an Everything Bagel Spice Chaffle and it was astonishing!! Today I had some remaining bacon in the ice chest that I chose to utilize.

They were so great and I think I have to twofold or triple the bunch so I can have more when I get eager!

They are so natural – blend the fixings, add them to the waffle producer, cook for 2:30 and it's finished!

This recipe makes 4 chaffles. You can place them in the ice chest and microwave them when you are ravenous.

I may likewise attempt to stick them into the toaster to perceive how they taste warmed.

Snap here to print the recipe for Keto bacon, egg, and cheddar Chaffles.

Keto Bacon, Egg, and Cheese Chaffles
2 eggs
3/4 cup cheddar
2 cuts cooked bacon

Guidelines:

Preheat your scaled down waffle creator. Splash with cooking oil.

Include the eggs and scramble them. Then include different fixings and blend well.

Pour 2 storing tablespoons of the hitter into the smaller than normal waffle creator.

Set a clock for 2:30 and pause.

When the time is done evacuate it with a fork. It will fresh us while you let it chill.

Discretionary – you can sprinkle some cheddar on to the egg blend before you close the waffle producer if you like additional cheddar season. It should give you that fresh cheddar enhance if you like that.

This chaffle breakfast sandwich meets up in under 10 minutes and makes eating keto or low carb diet a breeze! Just 3 Net Carbs for the entire sandwich!

The chaffle fever is as yet going solid and I love to think of different recipes that are fun and make the low carb or keto lifestyle a breeze! Breakfast sandwiches rush to make with chaffles because while the chaffle is cooking in your waffle iron, you can cook your egg in a skillet. Bacon or wiener patties can be cooked in the microwave so this entire whole breakfast sandwich meets up in less than 5 minutes. Judge me all you need yet that is the way I cook my bacon or wiener patties.

A chaffle is a waffle made of cheddar and an egg. It is essentially a play on consolidated words. There are various recipes for chaffles and some call for almond flour. I truly like the flavor of almond flour and that is the reason I add almond flour to my chaffles. A few people are hardcore chaffle fans and believe that a chaffle should just be an egg and cheddar. That is close to home inclination and one time somebody gave my chaffle recipe a low evaluating because of that. Entirely moronic as I would like to think however whatever I presume?

WHAT TYPE OF WAFFLE IRON SHOULD I USE?

I don't have a small scale waffle creator which is the thing that individuals are utilizing to make their chaffle buns or chaffle bread. I don't think a smaller than expected waffle iron is essential, however the scaled down waffles are pretty darn charming. I utilize my Villa waffle producer and afterward cut the chaffle down the middle to make a sandwich.

Run Mini Waffle Maker

Presto Ceramic FlipSide Waffle Maker

WHAT KIND OF CHEESE DO I NEED TO MAKE A CHAFFLE? Mozzarella or cheddar are the two cheeses that are well known to make chaffles with. I've seen individuals use Monterey jack. Pepper jack cheddar would be great if you like zesty chaffles.

Step by step instructions to MAKE A CHAFFLE BREAKFAST SANDWICH

Preheat your waffle iron.

While the waffle iron is preheating, combine the cheddar, egg, and almond flour together in a bowl.

Shower the waffle iron with Cooking Spray and spread the hitter on to the waffle iron. Close it and let the waffle cook.

While the waffle is cooking cook your egg in a skillet. Make whatever kind of egg you like. Cook bacon in microwave.

Collect your chaffle breakfast sandwich and appreciate.

FANCY ROSEMARY AND GOAT CHEESE PANINI

I experienced childhood with sandwiches; was raised on them, truth be told. My dark colored sack lunch, alongside a hard-bubbled egg and a creased pack of Fritos, constantly included one of the accompanying top choices: bologna and mayonnaise, fish serving of mixed greens and lettuce, nutty spread and two cuts of American cheddar, cream cheddar and pepperoni. These odd sandwiches, consistently on white bread, were little and level — and never contenders for lunch swapping. (I additionally adored egg plate of mixed greens, however even as an eight-year-old realized that bubbled egg yolks and mayonnaise putrefying in a coat storage room for a large portion of a day is a perilous move, socially.)

Be that as it may, my preferred sandwich never made it to class. It was one cut of Wonder bread, deliberately spread with a layer of Philadelphia cream cheddar and beat with Smuckers purple jam. The bread was then collapsed fifty-fifty like a taco and eaten while sitting on our scratchy plaid couch, Elvis cover over my knees, watching a recurrent scene of Little House on the Prairie.

This recipe is a riff on that after-school treat. We've supplanted the cream cheddar with new chèvre from Dirty Girl Farm in Andes and the Smuckers with Westwind Orchard's raspberry jam, yet it's still sweet and appetizing and makes for a terrific breakfast, lunch, or treat. Matched with a jug of shimmering white wine* and an off the cuff outing at Thorn Preserve, it's a balance of youth sentimentality and adult refinement.

*Hild Elbling is our preferred at the present time. It's lemony, scandalous, invigorating and, as its merchant claims, "sufficiently light to drink a whole container and still work overwhelming hardware."

Fixings 6 Servings

4 ounces goat cheddar, chèvre, softened

2 tablespoons milk

2 tablespoons McCormick Gourmet™ Organic Basil

2 teaspoons McCormick Gourmet™ Organic Rosemary, Crushed

1 teaspoon McCormick Gourmet™ Organic Garlic Powder
1 teaspoon McCormick Gourmet™ Organic Thyme
1 teaspoon McCormick Gourmet™ Sicilian Sea Salt
2 infant eggplant, cut longwise in 1/4-inch thick cuts
2 medium portobello mushrooms, cut in 1/2-inch thick cuts
1 medium fennel bulb, cut and cut the long way in 1/4-inch thick cuts
1 chayote, cut in 1/4-inch thick cuts Substitutions accessible
1 red ringer pepper, cut in 2-inch strips
1 little red onion, cut into 1/2-inch thick adjusts
1/3 cup olive oil
Crisply ground McCormick Gourmet™ Organic Black Peppercorns, Whole
1 portion Ciabatta bread, split down the middle on a level plane
1 cup arugula leaves, washed and depleted.

Directions

Blend goat cheddar, milk, basil, rosemary, garlic powder, thyme and 1/2 teaspoon of the ocean salt in medium bowl until all around mixed. Put in a safe spot. Delicately brush vegetables with oil. Season with staying 1/2 teaspoon ocean salt and pepper

Flame broil over medium-high warmth 5 to 10 minutes or until vegetables are delicate, turning once. Expel vegetables from flame broil and keep warm. Barbecue bread parts 30 seconds for every side or until gently toasted

Spread goat cheddar blend equitably over each bread half. Layer 1/2 of the arugula, flame broiled vegetables and remaining arugula on 1 bread half. Top with second bread half. Cut sandwich into 1/2-inch wide segments to serve.

CARLIC BRAD CHAFFLE

If you're in the mind-set for some keto-accommodating mushy bread, this keto chaffle recipe is actually what you're searching for.

You can dunk it in marinara sauce, use it instead of a low-carb bread recipe, make a keto pizza out of it, or simply appreciate them as it stands.

Don't hesitate to stir up the cheddar also, cheddar and parmesan work extraordinary. What's more, if you truly need to go for the garlicky flavor, you can top it with some garlic spread.

These low-carb garlic bread chaffles are:

Exquisite

Delightful

Firm

Tasty

garlic cheddar bread chaffles

The primary fixings are:

Immaculate Keto Unflavored Whey Protein

Egg

Almond flour

garlic cheddar bread chaffles

garlic cheddar bread chaffles

Discretionary extra fixings

Parmesan cheddar

Mozzarella cheddar

Coconut flour

garlic cheddar bread chaffles

3 Health Benefits of Garlic Cheese Bread Chaffles

garlic cheddar bread chaffles

#1: Promotes Weight Loss

If you will likely shed some weight, then getting enough protein is fundamental. This simple keto chaffle recipe evades carbs and handled fixings, yet it's wealthy in protein also.

Protein is the most satisfying macronutrient when contrasted with carbs and fat. In any case, whey protein, specifically, has been appeared to lessen craving by expanding a feeling of fulfillment and deferring the arrival of your appetite.

One examination found that contrasted with casein and a glucose control, whey protein significantly affected satiety and completion in overweight individuals.

#2: Supports Heart Health

With cardiovascular illness taking the main space for the main source of death in the U.S., it's no big surprise that heart health is top of psyche for such a large number of individuals.

Markers for coronary illness incorporate high blood lipids, aggravation, oxidation stress, and obviously — blood pressure.

While there are a lot of pharmaceuticals out there that are intended to battle these hazard factors, the appropriate response might be covering up in your kitchen wash room.

Garlic has been utilized for a huge number of years as a recuperating plant. Research shows that enhancing with garlic concentrate can decrease hypertension (pulse), and furthermore check oxidative pressure, accordingly offering cardioprotection to individuals with high blood pressure.

#3: Protects Your Cell Membranes

Almonds are a superb wellspring of nutrient E, a fat-dissolvable nutrient. Nutrient E assumes various jobs in your body however has an especially basic job in the security of your cells.

Each phone in your body is secured by a layer of fat, called the lipid bilayer. Nutrient E, with its fondness for fat, goes about as a cancer prevention agent and ensures this lipid bilayer.

The harming impacts of free radicals on your cells can add to a wide scope of issues, including cardiovascular ailment and malignant growth. Therefore, ensuring your phone films by getting enough nutrient E through your eating routine is imperative for prevention.

This mushy garlic bread chaffle is the ideal supplement to your preferred Italian dinners. You can serve it before as a little canapé, or make it part of the principle dish.

Not at all like most breadsticks and rolls that commonly go with your dinners, this flavorful chaffle is sans gluten and works flawlessly into your keto diet feast plan.

We simply made the BEST Cheesy Garlic Bread Chaffle Recipe ever! If you need a straightforward canapé that presents truly quick, make this recipe! It will even be appreciated by your non-keto companions! Truly, they will adore it as well!

The keto diet has been so great to me. It's stunning keto chaffle recipes like this that keep things intriguing. It scarcely feels like whatever ought to be known as an eating routine. It's a lifestyle... it is for me in any case. I don't figure I would have said that the initial 4 months into my voyage however... I recall strikingly that it was so difficult to begin and kick the sugar and carbs addictions I used to confront.

Gooey GARLIC BREAD CHAFFLE RECIPE INGREDIENTS (makes 2 gooey garlic bread chaffles)

Garlic Bread Chaffle Ingredients

1/2 cup mozzarella cheddar, destroyed

1 egg

1 tsp Italian flavoring

1/2 tsp garlic powder

1 tsp cream cheddar (I like to utilize seasoned cream cheddar, for example, chive and onion or jalapeno yet you can utilize plain as well)

Garlic Butter Topping Ingredients

1 tbs margarine

1/2 tsp Italian flavoring

1/2 tsp garlic powder

Mushy Bread Topping

2 tbs mozzarella cheddar, destroyed

run of parsley (or increasingly Italian flavoring)

Gooey GARLIC BREAD CHAFFLE RECIPE INSTRUCTIONS

Preheat your smaller than usual waffle producer.

Preheat your stove to 350F.

In a little bowl, combine the entirety of the garlic bread chaffle fixings until it's all around joined.

Separation the blend into equal parts and cook the first chaffle for at least 4 minutes. If you like you chaffles a piece crunchy outwardly, I would recommend you place a tsp of destroyed cheddar onto the waffle creator 30 seconds before including the chaffle fixings. This will make a pleasant, crunchy outside that is really astounding!

After you cook both of the garlic bread chaffles in the waffle creator, move them to a heating sheet.

In a different little bowl, dissolve the margarine in the microwave for around 10 seconds.

Add the garlic spread seasonings to the margarine blend.

Spread the margarine blend onto the warm chaffles with a treating brush.

Sprinkle a limited quantity of mozzarella over the garlic bread chaffles and afterward sprinkle with increasingly Italian flavoring.

Prepare for 5 minutes at 350F degrees. This is simply sufficient opportunity to soften the cheddar over the Cheesy Garlic Bread Chaffles!

Serve warm and appreciate them with a sugar free marinara sauce, for example, Rao's marinara sauce.

Simple Keto Cheesy Garlic Chaffle Bread will fulfill your yearnings for an Italian style bread that can be delighted in as a side or hors d'oeuvre. The divine gooey garlic goodness on a scrumptious crunchy chaffle meet up to make the best keto garlic chaffle bread you've at any point placed in your mouth.

Simple Keto Cheesy Garlic Chaffle Bread

A week ago I made one of my children's preferred suppers. They love spaghetti, and I welcome the way that it is a simple supper that we all appreciate, and I can make extra to cover lunch for a few days. My children make the most of their spaghetti meat sauce on noodles, while my better half and I love spaghetti squash. One of the children referenced that they would truly cherish it if I'd make garlic bread to go with their spaghetti and I in a split second idea of making a keto gooey garlic chaffle bread.

I realized it wouldn't be difficult to make as I could begin a group of chaffles while their noodles were cooking. The Keto Cheesy Garlic Chaffle Bread turned out superior to anything I envisioned with flavorful Italian flavoring and a delicious gooey garlic beating.

For what reason is it Called Chaffle Bread?

It appears as though medium-term, the chaffle advanced into the keto world in bunches all over Facebook, and it is digging in for the long haul. A chaffle is a cheddar waffle made of eggs and cheddar. Since it's underlying introduction in the keto low carb world, the chaffle recipe has extended to incorporate basically any blend of fixings, for example, destroyed cheddar, cream cheddar, overwhelming whipping cream, eggs, seasonings, preparing powder, keto-accommodating sugar, and other include ins. Essentially, it is made in the Dash Mini Waffle Makers, yet many change recipes to utilize a customary waffle iron or a smaller than expected waffle iron of a different brand. Most recipes I've seen are likewise sans gluten, yet I would twofold check all fixings first if you have a gluten hypersensitivity or affectability.

What do I Use to Make Keto Cheesy Garlic Chaffle Bread?

Run smaller than expected waffle creators happen to be the star of the chaffle appear, yet you could utilize any waffle producer that you as of now have. Remember that most chaffle recipes you see online are intended for the Dash Mini Waffle Maker, which makes a 4-inch chaffle, so you may need to alter the measure of hitter you use in an ordinary waffle iron and the cooking time.

Chaffle recipes typically make two cycle four-inch waffles. You do need to make each in turn, yet in under ten minutes you are set. Some bigger waffle irons may require more opportunity to cook the chaffle appropriately to get that pleasant brilliant darker shading.

If you have a major family or need to make a few without a moment's delay, this waffle creator makes four 3 inch waffles one after another. You would need to utilize somewhat less hitter, yet it would be a gigantic help.

Where Can I purchase the Dash Mini Waffle Maker?

Amazon Prime is my companion because items are conveyed to my entryway patio without me hauling my four children from store to store. That being stated, you might need to check Kohl's, Walmart, Target, Bed Bath and Beyond, or Sam's Club to check whether you can discover it coming up.

This chaffle bread recipe begins by tossing the entirety of the fixings recorded beneath in the recipe card in a little bowl.

Include simply enough player with the goal that it covers the base of the scramble smaller than normal creator. This recipe makes two chaffles. Try not to endeavor to pour the entirety of the player in on the double or you will have a wreck on your hands.

Keto Chaffle on a plate

I multiplied the recipe when I made this keto chaffle bread recipe with the goal that my whole family could appreciate it for supper. While it tasted delightful as may be, I realized it could be so much better.

What took it over the top is brushing the tops with a blend of softened margarine and garlic then sprinkling mozzarella cheddar on top. Then, I popped the Keto Cheesy Garlic Chaffle Bread in the broiler to dissolve the cheddar.

Sacred smokes, it was flavorful!! The cheddar was flawlessly liquefied, and the Italian flavors and garlic were on point. Don't hesitate to alter the flavors to suit your taste.

How to Serve Cheesy Garlic Chaffle?

Regardless of whether you serve the Keto Cheesy Garlic Bread Chaffle as a side to a dinner or a starter, it is a group pleaser. You can plunge the mushy garlic chaffle keto bread in a no additional sugar marinara as mezzetta Rao's, or ALDI natural brand. While I am certain there are other low carb sauces, those are the ones that I have by and by attempted and delighted in.

Would i be able to Make This Recipe Ahead of Time?

Of course, you can make this early and store either in the ice chest or the cooler. You'll need to rewarm in a manner with the goal that it crisps back up. Else, it will be delicate. You could utilize a toaster, air fryer, or wrap freely in foil in the stove to rewarm.

Chaffle recipes generally make two cycle four-inch waffles. You do need to make each in turn, yet in under ten minutes you are set. Some bigger waffle irons may require more opportunity to cook the chaffle appropriately to get that pleasant brilliant dark colored shading.

If you have a major family or need to make a few without a moment's delay, this waffle producer makes four 3 inch waffles one after another. You would need to utilize somewhat less player, yet it would be a tremendous help.

Where Can I purchase the Dash Mini Waffle Maker?

Amazon Prime is my companion because items are conveyed to my entryway patio without me hauling my four children from store to store. That being stated, you might need to check Kohl's, Walmart, Target, Bed Bath and Beyond, or Sam's Club to check whether you can discover it coming up.

run waffle producer and a bowl of hitter for the waffle

This chaffle bread recipe begins by tossing the entirety of the fixings recorded beneath in the recipe card in a little bowl.

waffle creator with player for Keto Chaffle

Include simply enough hitter with the goal that it covers the base of the scramble small producer. This recipe makes two chaffles. Try not to endeavor to pour the entirety of the hitter in without a moment's delay or you will have a wreck on your hands.

Keto Chaffle on a plate

I multiplied the recipe when I made this keto chaffle bread recipe with the goal that my whole family could appreciate it for supper. While it tasted flavorful as seems to be, I realized it could be so much better.

What took it over the top is brushing the tops with a blend of softened margarine and garlic then sprinkling mozzarella cheddar on top. Then, I popped the Keto Cheesy Garlic Chaffle Bread in the stove to dissolve the cheddar.

Blessed smokes, it was heavenly!! The cheddar was superbly dissolved, and the Italian flavors and garlic were on point. Don't hesitate to modify the flavors to suit your taste.

How to Serve Cheesy Garlic Chaffle?

Regardless of whether you serve the Keto Cheesy Garlic Bread Chaffle as a side to a feast or a canapé, it is a group pleaser. You can plunge the mushy garlic chaffle keto bread in a no additional sugar marinara as mezzetta Rao's, or ALDI natural brand. While I am certain there are other low carb sauces, those are the ones that I have actually attempted and appreciated.

Would i be able to Make This Recipe Ahead of Time?

Certainly, you can make this early and store either in the cooler or the cooler. You'll need to rewarm in a manner with the goal that it crisps back up. Else, it will be delicate. You could utilize a toaster, air fryer, or wrap freely in foil in the broiler to rewarm.

When you first expel the chaffle from the waffle creator it will be delicate and sort of feeble. Try to let it sit for a couple of moments. While it sits it solidifies a piece and is ideal for utilizing as keto bread or keto toast.

What is a Chaffle utilized for?

The fundamental chaffle recipe of egg and cheddar makes an awesome substitute for bread. Truth be told I like it better than my keto bagels and the 90 second keto bread.

From that point the conceivable outcomes are huge with what you can do with a chaffle. You can make a morning meal chaffle, chaffle sandwich, and even pastry chaffles!

What do I cook a chaffle in?

I have been cooking my chaffles in the Dash smaller than normal waffle creator. If you don't have a smaller than normal waffle iron you can snatch one on amazon. They are amazing and absolutely spending well disposed. The fundamental chaffle recipe will make 2 chaffles in a little waffle creator.

You can likewise utilize an ordinary measured waffle creator you make keto chaffle recipes. When utilizing a typical measured waffle producer the fundamental keto chaffle recipe it will make 1 chaffle.

If you have many individuals in your home, consider getting this waffle producer that will make 4 keto waffles at the same time!

BAKED POTATO LOW CARB CHAFFLE

Heavenly Moly! This Baked Potato Chaffle is AMAZING! If you miss potatoes on the Keto diet, you are going to cherish this Keto chaffle recipe!

Heavenly Moly! This Jicama Loaded Baked Potato Chaffle is AMAZING! If you miss potatoes on the Keto diet, you are going to cherish this Keto chaffle recipe! Gigantic because of Cheryl W. from the Keto Chaffle Recipes Group for imparting these astounding recipes to us!

BAKED POTATO CHAFFLE RECIPE INGREDIENTS

1 enormous jicama root

1/2 medium onion, minced

2 garlic cloves, squeezed

1 cup cheddar of decision (I utilized Halloumi)

2 eggs, whisked

Salt and Pepper

Heated POTATO CHAFFLE RECIPE INSTRUCTIONS

Strip jicama and shred in nourishment processor

Spot destroyed jicama in an enormous colander, sprinkle with 1-2 tsp of salt. Blend well and permit to deplete.

Press out however much fluid as could reasonably be expected (significant advance)

Microwave for 5-8 minutes

Combine all fixings

Sprinkle a little cheddar on waffle iron before including 3 T of the blend, sprinkle somewhat more cheddar over the blend

Cook for 5 minutes. Flip and cook 2 more.

Top with a bit of harsh cream, bacon pieces, cheddar, and chives!

What is a jicama?

Jicama root is a round root vegetable local to Mexico that has a surface like a potato. It's low in calories and high in indispensable supplements. Jicama has around 5 net carbs per 100g. Jicama is stacked with fiber, nutrient c, and potassium! It additionally contains insoluble fiber.

If you haven't encountered jicama in your feasting collection, you have everything to pick up — and if you're wanting to shed some overabundance pounds, this may be your new top pick.

DESSERTS

SUGAR COOKIE CHAFFLES

WOWZERS! Take a gander at this Chocolate Chip Cookie Chaffle Cake Recipe!! This is another Cheryl mixture of chaffle yet she utilized the chocolate chip treat recipe found in the Keto Friendly Recipes cookbook!!! How cool is that?!! There are huge amounts of recipes in that cookbook that can be made in the waffle producer. Actually, the chaffle recipe base fixings are the same old thing. Keto individuals have been making a cheddar based bread for quite a while now. Go to page 30 of that book and you will see the Jalapeno Cheese Bread recipe that uses the base recipe fixings that are precisely the same as the base for the fundamental chaffle recipe fixings.

In any case, this Chocolate Chip Cookie Chaffle Cake Recipe is astounding! This IS the thing that Low Carb dreams are made of! Keto dreams that is!

Update: This recipe made it to this rundown of BEST Chaffle Recipes on the web! If you love chaffles, you will see that rundown as overly accommodating!

Elements for cake layers:

1 tablespoon spread, dissolved

1 tablespoon Golden Monkfruit sugar

1 egg yolk

1/8 teaspoon vanilla concentrate

1/8 teaspoon cake player remove

3 tablespoons almond flour

1/8 teaspoon heating powder

1 tablespoon chocolate chips, sugar free

Whipped Cream Frosting Ingredients:

1 teaspoon unflavored gelatin

4 teaspoon cold water

1 cup substantial whipping cream

2 tablespoons confectioners' sugar

WHY IS IT CALLED A CHAFFLE?

It's known as a chaffle because cheddar + waffles = Chaffles! It's only a shrewd name that somebody in the keto network designed. Truly adorable, huh?!!

WHAT KITCHEN GADGET DO YOU USE TO MAKE CHAFFLES?

I love my little Mini Waffle Maker and I use it constantly. You can utilize a full-size waffle creator, simply be certain you twofold the recipe much of the time.

Would you be able to FREEZE CHAFFLES?

Truly, they hold up well! Simply make certain to wrap them firmly in a sealed shut holder to keep them new more. You can freeze them for as long as a month. I haven't tried any more extended than that.

Would you be able to MAKE CHAFFLES FOR A WHOLE WEEK AT ONE TIME?

You can likewise prepare early and make new chaffles for the week. They will remain new as long as you keep them refrigerated. To warm them, basically pop them in the microwave or air fryer to warm them up. The air fryer will in general get them pleasant and firm if that is the thing that you are going for!

This Pumpkin Chaffle Keto Sugar Cookies Recipe is ideal for fall. Sweet, chewy and delicate, these keto sugar treats have everything!

This Pumpkin Chaffle Keto Sugar Cookies Recipe is ideal for fall. Sweet, chewy and delicate, these keto sugar treats have everything!

Keto Chaffle Recipe eBook Cookbook

Keto Chaffle Recipes digital book

Keto Chaffle Recipes digital book

Searching FOR KETO CHAFFLE RECIPES? HERE YA GO!!!!

We have all the best keto chaffle recipes with new recipes being made day by day! In our new, Keto Chaffle Recipes eBook Cookbook, you will get over 50+ sweet and exquisite keto recipes for each flavor palette.

Essential Chaffle Recipes

Appetizing Chaffle Recipes

Sweet Chaffle Recipes

Chaffle Cake Recipes

CHOCOLATE CHIP COOKIE CHAFFLE

CHOCOLATE CHIP CHAFFLES are the least difficult contort on the most recent low carb furor, yet those small amounts of chocolate covering up all through the waffle are mystical. We serve our own with a major touch of whipped cream, however some low carb frozen yogurt would be a scrumptious garnish for dessert!

Keto Chocolate Chip Waffles! Only 3 net carbs per serving! #lowcarb #keto #chaffles #waffles

Indeed, it's legitimate.

Chocolate Chip Chaffles

I have been making a different sort of chaffle each and every day since I found them and in addition to the fact that i am snared... my family is as well!

My girl requested a little chaffle exercise at the beginning of today with the goal that she could make her own for breakfast. Also, no, she's not low carb and truly, we do really have a case of Eggos in the cooler for her to snatch on occupied mornings.

If that doesn't disclose to you how great chaffles are, well, I don't have a clue what will. You're simply must attempt them for yourself!

Haven't caught wind of the chaffle rage yet? Snap here for every one of the subtleties and the essential recipe!

These chocolate chip chaffles are very basic with only a bunch of fixings and they're prepared in minutes. We serve these keto waffles at breakfast with whipped cream or for dessert with a scoop of low carb frozen yogurt!

low carb chocolate chip waffles with whipped cream

The most effective method to make keto waffles with chocolate chips:

This post contains member joins.

You're going to require an egg, some finely destroyed mozzarella cheddar (simply trust me), a little coconut flour, sugar, vanilla, and some without sugar chocolate chips.

I utilize and prescribe Lakanto Monkfruit for the sugar. It's a mix of erythritol and monkfruit which disposes of any lingering flavor and it's everything characteristic as well! Use code THATLOWCARBLIFE for 20% off your whole request.

Whisk together your egg, coconut flour, sugar, and vanilla and afterward mix in the cheddar.

chaffle player

This looks somewhat out of control, yet you simply must have confidence that I wouldn't lead you off track.

Spoon half of the hitter into your smaller than normal waffle iron and afterward speck the top with chocolate chips. Utilize a spoon to spread a touch of hitter of the chips so they don't consume when you close the waffle iron.

step by step instructions to make chocolate chip waffles

Close the iron and cook for 3-4 minutes, contingent upon how fresh you'd like your waffles.

Rehash with the remainder of the hitter, stack them up, and squirt on some whipped cream.

Breakfast is served!

This Chocolate Chip Chaffle Keto recipe is fast and simple to make. Loaded with low carb chocolate chips, it has quite recently enough chocolate goodness to fulfill yearnings when you need a simple keto dessert while following the ketogenic diet.

chocolate chip chaffle keto recipe plated with whipped cream and sugar free chocolate chips on top

Chocolate Chip Chaffle Dessert Recipe

As I had referenced previously, the Keto Chaffle has overwhelmed the keto world as of late. You'll discover varieties of recipes all over keto facebook bunches that incorporate both sweet and exquisite choices. Some keto chaffle recipes are made with simply cheddar and eggs, while different recipes have dared to different fixings and mixes. This Chocolate Chip Chaffle keto recipe is made with only a couple of fixings. I tried it a few times to get it without flaw. Topped with a little sans sugar whipped beating, it makes a tasty keto low carb dessert.

The first recipe is just eggs and cheddar, which is essentially a cheddar waffle. Yet, since the chaffle was brought it has blossomed into a wide range of recipes that are alluded to as a chaffle paying little respect to the fixings. It appears that most exquisite chaffle recipes use cheddar destroyed cheddar while the sweet chaffle recipes use mozzarella cheddar rather because of the mellow flavor or different fixings rather than cheddar.

What kitchen apparatus do I requirement for this Chocolate Chip Chaffle Keto Recipe?

Run smaller than normal waffle creators have turned into a web sensation nearby the chaffle recipe. This smaller than expected waffle iron makes flawless 4-inch waffles and they are very reasonable. I love that they don't occupy a great deal of room in my kitchen and can without much of a stretch be put away in the cupboard. I don't care for a ton of fastidious apparatuses that occupy counter or cupboard room so this keto waffle creator for chaffles is great.

Most recipes you find for Chaffles, regardless of whether sweet or exquisite, make two four-inch chaffles.

For those of you who might want to make a few without a moment's delay for some other time, or have a major family like me, this waffle creator might be a superior decision as you can make four 3-inch chaffles immediately time.

Where Can I purchase the Dash Mini Waffle Maker?

Amazon has a few different Dash scaled down waffle producers accessible in different hues. Obviously, you could search for one in stores, for example, TJMaxx, Kohl's, Target, or Walmart however I've perused that many are sold out.

Begin with a little bowl for this chaffle keto recipe. You'll include the entirety of the fixings and afterward consolidate well. I've perused that a few people utilize a drenching blender or an enchantment projectile to blend the entirety of the fixings. This chocolate chip chaffle keto recipe makes two chaffles. If you attempt to utilize the entirety of the player for one, the hitter will dribble out of the waffle producer all over the place.

I use sans sugar Lily's chocolate, which is viewed as endorsed keto chocolate for the keto diet. Lily's chocolate chips are improved with stevia.

Tip: Instead of blending the chocolate contributes the keto chaffle hitter, I sprinkled them on top so they wouldn't all sink to the base.

The heating powder in Chocolate Chip Chaffles keto recipe encourages the chaffles to puff up with the goal that they are less thick. I cook dig for 3-4 minutes until they are brilliant dark colored. Else, they will adhere to the waffle producer a piece. After you expel from the waffle creator, put in a safe spot for a couple of moments as they will fresh as they chill off.

You could appreciate this Chocolate Chip Chaffle keto recipe with without sugar whipped besting or with sans sugar maple syrup if wanted.

Are Keto Chaffles Gluten-Free?

As a mother of a kid with serious nourishment sensitivities, I generally encourage every individual to check the fixings and names of the careful fixings you use in your kitchen. While the fixings would be without gluten in principle, it is in every case best to twofold check for yourself.

Would i be able to Freeze Chocolate Chip Keto Dessert Chaffles?

Indeed, they can be solidified in a cooler safe holder or wrapped exclusively. I would recommend rewarming in the broiler enclosed by aluminum foil or an air fryer as they won't be firm generally.

Varieties to this recipe:

Include a tsp of cream cheddar to the player for included flavor Swap out coconut flour for almond flour. Coconut flour and almond flour are not a 1:1 substitution. By and large, the substitution is 1 section coconut flour to 4 sections almond flour, yet I have perused that in this recipe it is nearer to 1:3.

Swerve can be utilized rather than Lakanto Monkfruit, and the estimation is the equivalent.

More Chaffle Keto Recipes:

Profoundly Popular Traditional Keto Chaffle Recipe
The Very Best Pizza Chaffle Recipe
Maple Pumpkin Chaffle Keto Recipe
Taco Chaffle Recipe
Blueberry Keto Chaffle with almond flour
Little Keto Pizza with Chaffle Pizza Crust
Keto Chaffle Breakfast Sandwich with almond flour

The most effective method to Make Chocolate Chip Chaffle Keto Recipe:

Keto Chocolate Chip Chaffle Keto Recipe

This heavenly keto Chocolat Chip Chaffle Dessert Recipe is anything but difficult to make and tastes delightful. You can prepare a bunch in minutes to appreciate.

Planning Time

5 mins

Cook Time

8 mins

Course: bread, Breakfast, Dessert

Food: American, easygoing

Watchword: chaffle dessert, chaffle keto recipe, chocolate chip chaffle

Servings: 1Calories: 146kcalAuthor: Kasey Trenum

Fixings

1 egg

1 tbsp overwhelming whipping cream

1/2 tsp coconut flour

1 3/4 tsp Lakanto monkfruit brilliant can utilize pretty much to alter sweetness

1/4 tsp preparing powder

touch of salt

1 tbsp Lily's Chocolate Chips

Directions

Turn on the waffle creator with the goal that it warms up.

In a little bowl, consolidate all fixings with the exception of the chocolate chips and mix well until joined.

Oil waffle creator, then pour half of the hitter onto the base plate of the waffle producer. Sprinkle a couple of chocolate chips on top and afterward close.

Cook for 3-4 minutes or until the chocolate chip chaffle pastry is brilliant darker then expel from waffle producer with a fork, being mindful so as not to consume your fingers.

Rehash with the remainder of the hitter.

Let chaffle sit for a couple of moments so it starts to fresh. If wanted present with without sugar whipped besting.

Notes

The sugar alcohols from the Lakanto Monkfruit Golden are excluded from the healthful data since most subtract to figure net carbs.

Nourishment

Serving: 1g | Calories: 146kcal | Carbohydrates: 7g | Protein: 6g | Fat: 10g | Saturated Fat: 7g | Fiber: 3g | Sugar: 1g

GINGERBREAD

An immortal, exemplary, conventional Gingerbread recipe! This is one of my family's preferred recipes. It makes for a thick however delicate, clammy, and luxuriously seasoned gingerbread, impeccably enhanced with molasses, dark colored sugar, and heaps of comfortable flavors!

Not to be mistaken for gingerbread treats, this cake is so easy to whip together. Make a point to finish yours off with a spot of hand crafted whipped cream! Recipe incorporates a how-to video at the base of the post!

Cut of gingerbread bested with whipped cream

Possibly you've seen at this point almost the entirety of my family most loved recipes begin from a similar source. My preferred Angel Food Cake, Chocolate Fudge, and now this Gingerbread recipe all start from my mother's amazingly exhausted Good Housekeeping cookbook.

Furthermore, that book is super, exhausted, as well. The coupling has actually been conduit taped together now. Each time you open it, pages vacillate out and onto the floor. The most well-adored pages are shrouded in chocolate and molasses stains. It is presumably the most well-utilized cookbook I've at any point known, and in light of current circumstances. The recipes within it are works of art, and they're super great.

I realized that I needed to share a Gingerbread recipe for these special seasons, however an extraordinary recipe, I needed it to be this one.

Cut of gingerbread recipe with a chomp out of it

A CLASSIC GINGERBREAD RECIPE

My mother makes this recipe often and it never keeps going long. It's so easy to make, is lavishly enhanced with molasses and conventional gingerbread flavors, and it turns out superbly every. single. time.

I made a couple of minor changes to this recipe to make it my own. After a couple of recipe trials, I concluded that I wanted to utilize spread as opposed to the shortening that the recipe called for initially (and I suggest utilizing European margarine, if you can get your hands on it). I likewise exchanged out white sugar for dim dark colored sugar for considerably a greater amount of that rich molasses season.

Ensure that you use unsulphured molasses for this gingerbread. I generally utilize Grandma's image because that is the thing that my supermarket conveys, and it says "unsulphured" directly on the name.

Gingerbread hitter

Gingerbread hitter, all set into the broiler

Gingerbread turns out overwhelming, yet each nibble is splendidly enhanced and soggy and just melts in your mouth. This is the ideal comfortable wintertime treat.

I prescribe serving your Gingerbread while it's still warm as opposed to holding on to enable it to cool totally. Try not to misunderstand me, the scraps are unbelievable, however there's simply something so scrumptious about still-warm gingerbread.

My kin and I constantly finished our own off with Cool Whip, yet now that I'm more established and more shrewd I just utilize my custom made whipped cream recipe. A Major scoop of vanilla frozen yogurt would likewise be an incredible blending, since I'm considering it.

Appreciate!

MORE RECIPES YOU MAY ENJOY:

Gingerbread Cupcakes

Molasses Cookies

Gingerbread Fudge

Gingerbread Layer Cake

The most effective method to MAKE GINGERBREAD

Make certain to look at my Gingerbread Recipe VIDEO just underneath the recipe! If you appreciate these recordings, if it's not too much trouble consider buying in to my YouTube Channel so you can be the first to see the entirety of my cooking recordings <3

Gingerbread

An exemplary gingerbread recipe! Firmly adjusted from Good Housekeeping (offshoot).

4.88 from 31 votes

Print Pin Rate

Course: DessertCuisine: AmericanKeyword: christmas recipe, gingerbread, occasion heating, recipe with molassesPrep Time: 20 minutesCook Time: 45 minutesTotal Time: 1 hour 5 minutesServings: 9 enormous slicesCalories: 400kcalAuthor: Sam Merritt

Fixings

½ cup unsalted margarine (ideally European spread) softened to room temperature (113g)

½ cup dim darker sugar firmly stuffed (100g)

1 cup unsulphured molasses (235ml) (I utilize Grandma's image)

1 huge egg

1 teaspoon vanilla concentrate

2 ½ cups generally useful flour (312g)

1 ½ teaspoon preparing pop

1 teaspoon ground cinnamon

1 teaspoon ground ginger

½ teaspoon ground cloves

¾ teaspoon salt

1 cup bubbling water (235ml)

Whipped Cream for fixing, discretionary

Guidelines

Preheat broiler to 350F (175C) and set up a 9"x9" preparing dish by either liberally lubing and flouring or by fixing with material paper. Put in a safe spot.

Join spread and dark colored sugar in an enormous bowl and utilize an electric blender to beat until velvety.

Include molasses and mix until very much consolidated.

Include egg and vanilla concentrate. Mix well.

In a different bowl, whisk together flour, preparing pop, ground cinnamon, ground ginger, ground cloves, and salt.

Step by step add dry fixings to wet until totally consolidated.

Cautiously mix in bubbling water until fixings are smooth and well-consolidated.

Empty hitter into arranged preparing container and heat on 350F (175C) for 40 minutes or until a toothpick embedded in the inside tells the truth or with a couple of clammy scraps.

Permit to cool before cutting and serving. This Gingerbread tastes best when topped with whipped cream!

The most effective method to make gingerbread bread rolls:

Include spread, brilliant syrup and light dark colored sugar to a dish. Mix on a low warmth until sugar has broken up.

Include flour, bicarbonate of pop and ginger to a combining bowl then mix. Make a well in the middle and pour in the sugar and margarine blend.

Mix together to frame a mixture (it may be most effortless to utilize your hands).

Enclose by clingfilm and let chill for 30mins to solidify.

Lay the batter between two sheets of heating material. Press mixture delicately with a moving pin. Give a quarter turn than rehash.

Give it a last quarter turn, then begin to move in reverse and advances, giving ordinary quarter turns. Until batter is generally thickness of a £1 coin.

Utilizing a scone shaper cut out the shapes. Heat at 190°C (170°C fan) mark 5 for 10 to 12min, until gently brilliant dark colored.

The bread rolls won't be firm however will solidify when left to cool outside the broiler.

BOSTOM CREAM PIE CHAFFLE

Fixings
Chaffle Cake Ingredients:
2 eggs
1/4 cup almond flour
1 tsp coconut flour
2 tbsp liquefied spread
2 tbsp cream cheddar room temp
20 drops Boston Cream remove
1/2 tsp vanilla concentrate
1/2 tsp heating powder
2 tbsp swerve confectioners' sugar or monkfruit
1/4 tsp Xanthan powder
Custard Ingredients:
1/2 cup substantial whipping cream
1/2 tsp Vanilla concentrate
1/2 tbs Swerve confectioners Sweetener
2 Egg Yolks
1/8 tsp Xanthan Gum
Ganache Ingredients:
2 tbs substantial whipping cream
2 tbs Unsweetened Baking chocolate bar slashed
1 tbs Swerve Confectioners Sweetener

Boston Cream Pie gets a keto makeover! I as of late refreshed this low carb formula and now it's shockingly better than previously, with less carbs. Delicate almond flour cake loaded up with sugar free vanilla cake cream and a rich low carb chocolate coat.

Keto Boston Cream Pie formula - a cut of the cake on white plate with raspberries, with the remainder of the cake on a white cake remain out of sight

I lived in the Boston territory for more than 11 years and the first occasion when I at any point attempted this exemplary cake was the point at which I made my very own low carb form, route back in October of 2011. Given that it's the city's legitimate treat (as indicated by the ever solid Wikipedia), it's very astounding that I never gave this delightful pastry the hour of day. Try not to commit a similar error I did, my companions! Make this Boston Cream Pie formula when you can and you will be happy you did.

IS IT A PIE OR A CAKE?

On the off chance that you've at any point been to Boston, you will know exactly how confounding that city it, with its wandering roads and absence of good road signs. Potentially you even approached somebody for headings and got very convoluted, attempting to understand their multi-step guidelines. Trust me when I state that driving around that town isn't for the swoon of heart. Any of you who have ever determined on Storrow Drive know precisely what I am discussing!

Indeed, with regards to the Bostonian method for making things confounding, Boston Cream Pie isn't a pie by any stretch of the imagination, yet actually a cake. A cake loaded up with vanilla baked good cream and bested with chocolate. OK, so it might appear as though they are purposely attempting to perplex pariahs with ill-advised names and poor road signage, yet with regards to dessert, Bostonians aren't messing around! You can't generally turn out badly with a custard-filled cake beat with delicious chocolate ganache. Since I've made my own and tasted it, it's very stunning I never did it.

Refreshed BOSTON CREAM PIE RECIPE

My unique low carb formula was in line with a peruser, wayyyyyyy in 2011. Kid that appears to be a quite a while back! Indeed, even in those days, I was really deft at low carb heating and it was generally simple to make sense of how to make over this great cake and decrease the sugar and carbs. Be that as it may, in the course of recent years, I have sharpened my keto preparing aptitudes , so the time had come to handle a little update.

—

For a certain something, the cornstarch in the vanilla cake cream needed to go. That isn't something I use at all any longer and I've discovered that thickener or glucomannan work much better as a keto thickener. I additionally added an additional egg yolk to help thicken the cream filling.

Be that as it may, regardless I thought that it was a piece on the goopy side so I sped in only a dash of coconut flour with the goal that it didn't overflow out a lot between my cake layers. You may discover you needn't bother with it, contingent upon how well your cake cream thickens up.

I decreased the carbs in the cake layers also, by utilizing my standard vanilla cake formula yet by subbing out one of the cups of almond flour for a 1/3 cup of coconut flour.

Next up I handled the coating. I used to make a chocolate coat that was situated in spread yet I've discovered that I can really make a great keto chocolate ganache the conventional way, by stewing cream and afterward liquefying the chocolate in the cream. Obviously I can't utilize chocolate with sugar, so I utilize unsweetened chocolate and race in a little sugar toward the end. The thickness of your chocolate coating will depend a little on the brand of cocoa powder you use (I utilized Rodelle). This is the reason I've likewise included directions for diminishing or thickening the coating as vital.

Single cut of Boston Cream Pie on a white plate with raspberries, encompassed by greenish blue gauzy texture

THE RESULTS

Truly the refreshed Boston Cream Pie formula and the old adaptation are both great and they taste about the equivalent. The two of them have a velvety focus and a rich chocolate coat. Furthermore, goodness, is there anything prettier than chocolate ganache trickling down the sides of a cake? I think not! In any case, this new formula is easier and increasingly clear. What's more, it avoids the yucky fixings like cornstarch, so you realize this will fit in well with your keto diet.

I took this to a companion's home for a finish of-summer grill and it was eaten up by everybody! You know it's great when even the non-low carbers give it rave audits.

BANANA NUT CHAFFLES

I simply made the BEST Banana Nut Chaffle Recipe I've at any point attempted! Omgosh, It's stunning!

Here's the mystery fixing however... You can't do bananas on the keto diet. They are truly elevated carb so you need to stay away from them however much as could be expected. In the event that you love the flavor of banana, you completely should get some banana remove! It's a distinct advantage! I utilize the Lorann Banana Extract here. There are huge amounts of great banana separate brands you can get. Here are a couple of we would prescribe:

Next, you completely need a small waffle creator! Run makes the best! Presently, you needn't bother with the scaled down however you do require a waffle creator. In the event that you have a full-size waffle producer, you can totally utilize that however simply ensure you twofold the formula!

BANANA NUT CHAFFLE RECIPE INGREDIENTS

1 egg

1 tbs cream cheddar. relaxed and room temp

1 tbs sugar free cheesecake pudding (discretionary fixing since it is messy keto)

1/2 cup mozzarella cheddar

1 tbs Monkfruit confectioners

1/4 tsp vanilla concentrate

1/4 tsp banana remove

Discretionary Toppings:

Sugar free caramel sauce (we have a natively constructed caramel sauce form here: How to Make Sugar Free Caramel Sauce)

Walnuts (or any of your preferred nuts)

BANANA NUT CHAFFLE RECIPE INSTRUCTIONS

Preheat the small scale waffle creator

In a little bowl, whip the egg.

Add the rest of the fixings to the egg blend and blend it until it's very much fused.

Add a large portion of the player to the waffle creator and cook it for at least 4 minutes until it's brilliant darker.

Evacuate the completed chaffle and include the other portion of the hitter to cook the other chaffle.

Top with your discretionary fixings and serve warm!

Do despite everything you have days that you search for comfort nourishment? We understand now, that the best nourishments are sound decisions. Our most up to date go-to formula is a Chaffle. What is a Chaffle you inquire? A Chaffle is the ideal blending of cheddar and an egg cooked in a waffle creator. Truly, you heard that right. This is a distinct advantage and it has surprised the keto world.

(As an Amazon Associate we gain from qualifying buys. This post may contain subsidiary connections. Snap here to find out additional.)

The essential Chaffle formula is basically cheddar and egg. We, obviously, have made it a stride further and idealized the formula with the expansion of only a couple of more fixings. Furthermore, the best part, it just takes a few minutes to get ready.

Chaffle Ham Sandwich

The Chaffle can be utilized for burger buns, wiener buns, tortillas, Monte Cristos, pizza, and even treats. Also, it doesn't stop there. Think about the potential outcomes! Exactly when we figure we can't adore this keto way of life any longer, along comes the Chaffle. This is our form of the Chaffle formula. So proceed, Chaffle on.

The fundamental formula makes 2 little Chaffles. Serving size is both Chaffles. These plans can be multiplied or even significantly increased. You can refrigerate them or even freeze them.

Fixings:

1/2 cup of cheddar, destroyed (you can utilize any cheddar)

1 egg

1 tsp of sans gluten preparing powder

2 tablespoons of almond flour (can substitute with 1 tablespoon of coconut flour whenever wanted)

Guidelines:

Assemble and set up the entirety of your fixings and preheat your waffle creator.

Combine your egg, destroyed cheddar, heating powder, and almond or coconut flour.

Empty a large portion of your blend into the waffle producer. Cook till done. Expel. Empty the rest of the hitter into the waffle creator and cook.

We purchased the little Dash brand smaller than normal waffle creator and the scaled down frying pan (you can utilize it is possible that one) to use with this formula and it makes the ideal size Chaffle. Try not to have a small scale waffle creator? You can utilize a normal waffle producer or skillet after all other options have been exhausted.

Chaffle Variations

For every variety, you will consolidate the fixings recorded at that point cook similarly as you would the essential Chaffle formula. When cooking chaffle just add roughly 2 to 2 1/2 tablespoons of player to the smaller than normal waffle producer. In the event that you are utilizing a customary size waffle producer split the hitter down the middle.

These varieties make 3 to 4 servings.

Bacon Chaffle

1 egg
1/2 cup cheddar, destroyed
2 Tbsp almond flour
1 tsp heating powder
3 Tbsp cooked bacon disintegrates

Blueberry Muffin Chaffle
1/2 cup of mozzarella cheddar, destroyed

1 egg
1 tsp of heating powder
2 tablespoons of almond flour
2 tsp of sugar
Bunch of blueberries
2 tablespoon of slashed nuts (discretionary)

Blueberry Muffin Chaffle

Cinnamon Roll Chaffle
1/2 cup of mozzarella cheddar, destroyed
1 egg
1 tsp of heating powder

2 tablespoons of almond flour
1 to 2 tsp of cinnamon
1 tsp of vanilla
1 tsp of sugar
Nut Butter Chaffle
1 egg
1/2 cup mozzarella cheddar
1 tsp vanilla
1 tablespoon sugar
2 Tbsp nut margarine
1/2 tsp of heating powder
2 tablespoons of almond flour
Top with natively constructed whipping cream for a treat.
Nut Butter Chaffle Stack
Lemon Delight Chaffle
1 oz cream cheddar (relaxed)
1/4 cup mozzarella cheddar, destroyed
1 egg
1 to 2 tsp lemon juice
2 tablespoons of sugar
1 tsp heating powder
4 tablespoons of almond flour
This is extraordinary with some cream cheddar icing.
Lemon Delight Chaffle
Banana Nut Muffin Chaffle
1 oz cream cheddar (mellowed)
1/4 cup mozzarella cheddar, destroyed
1 egg
1 tsp banana remove
2 tablespoons of sugar
1 tsp preparing powder
4 tablespoons of almond flour
2 tablespoons of pecans or walnuts, cleaved
Banana Nut Chaffle
Pizza Chaffle
1 egg
1/2 cup cheddar, destroyed
1 Tbsp keto inviting marinara sauce
2 Tbsp pepperoni (cut into little pieces)

---

1 tsp of preparing powder
4 tablespoon almond flour
1 tsp of Italian flavoring
These are incredible topped with parmesan cheddar.

Oreo Chaffle

1 egg
1/2 cup of mozzarella cheddar, destroyed
1/2 tsp of preparing powder
2 tablespoons of cacao powder
2 tablespoons of sugar
2 tablespoon of almond flour
These are incredible topped with cream cheddar icing.

McGriddle Chaffle

1 egg
1 oz cream cheddar, mollified
1 tsp sugar
1 tsp vanilla
1 tablespoon keto-accommodating maple syrup (We use Lakanto)
1/4 cup mozzarella cheddar, destroyed
1 tsp of preparing powder
4 tablespoons of almond flour

Chaffle McGriddle Sandwich

Chocolate Dream Chaffle

1 egg
1/4 cup of mozzarella cheddar
1 oz cream cheddar
2 tsp sugar
2 tablespoons cacao powder
1 tsp vanilla
4 Tbsp almond flour
1 tsp preparing powder

Red Velvet Chaffle

1 egg
1/4 cup of mozzarella cheddar
1 oz cream cheddar
2 tsp sugar
2 tablespoons cacao powder
1 tsp red velvet concentrate

4 Tbsp almond flour
1 tsp heating powder
This is so great with some cream cheddar icing.
ChaffleTortillas
1 egg
1/2 cup cheddar, destroyed
4 tablespoon of almond flour
1 tsp heating powder
1/2 to 1 tablespoon of almond milk or substantial whipping cream
1/4 tsp of garlic powder
Chaffle Tortilla
We make these in a skillet rather than the waffle creator with the goal that we can get them looking like a tortilla.
Macros:
Fundamental Chaffle Recipe
Serving Size: 1 serving (2 Chaffles)
Supplement
Calories
Net Carbs
Fiber
Protein
Fat
All out Carbs Value
380
2.0 g
2.0 g
22 g
31 g
5.0 g

CARROT CAKE CHAFFLE

Basic exemplary flavor in a waffle cake structure total with delicious cream cheddar icing. This is my life partner's most mentioned cake and now he can have it low carb!

? I'm not going to mislead anybody, I licked the bowl! ?

CARROT CHAFFLE CAKE RECIPE INGREDIENTS

Carrot Chaffle Cake fixings

1/2 cup carrot, destroyed

1 egg

2 T spread, liquefied

2 T overwhelming whipping cream

3/4 cup almond flour

1 T pecans, cleaved

2 T powdered sugar

2 tsp cinnamon

1 tsp pumpkin flavor

1 tsp preparing powder

Cream Cheese Frosting

4 oz cream cheddar, mellowed

1/4 cup powdered sugar

1 tsp vanilla concentrate

1-2 T substantial whipping cream (contingent upon the consistency you like)

CARROT CHAFFLE CAKE RECIPE INSTRUCTIONS

Blend your dry fixings – almond flour, cinnamon, pumpkin zest, heating powder, powdered sugar, and pecan pieces.

Include the wet fixings ground carrot, egg, dissolved spread, overwhelming cream.

Add 3 T hitter to preheated small waffle creator. Cook 2 1/2 – 3 minutes.

Combine icing fixings with a hand blender with whisk connection until all around consolidated.

Stack waffles and include icing between each layer!

CARROT CHAFFLE CAKE RECIPE NUTRITION INFORMATION

Makes 6 Chaffles. (Servings) 2.4 net carbs without icing. 3.7 net carbs with icing. 1/4 of cake is 5.5 net carbs!

STRAWBERRY SHORTCAKE CHAFFLE

I simply made the most brilliant Strawberry Shortcake Chaffle Recipe! OMGosh, you must attempt it! The introduction for this sweet keto-accommodating pastry was additional uncommon as well! We acquired these charming minimal individual size cake plates only for these pastry chaffles! Did you see the charming Pumpkin Cake Chaffle Recipe we posted not long ago! It's gone insane viral and everybody is adoring that formula!

STRAWBERRY SHORTCAKE CHAFFLE RECIPE INGREDIENTS

1 egg

1/4 cup mozzarella cheddar

1 tbs cream cheddar

1/4 tsp heating powder

2 strawberries, cut

1 tsp strawberry separate STRAWBERRY SHORTCAKE CHAFFLE RECIPE INSTRUCTIONS

Preheat waffle producer.

In a little bowl, whip the egg.

Include the rest of the fixings.

Shower the waffle producer with nonstick cooking splash.

Gap blend fifty-fifty.

Cook a large portion of the blend for around 4 minutes or until brilliant dark colored.

STRAWBERRY SHORTCAKE CHAFFLE RECIPE NUTRITION LABEL INFORMATION

(this does exclude the garnishes, just the chaffle) Makes 2 chaffles.

Discretionary Glaze: 1 tbs cream cheddar warmed in the microwave for 15 seconds, 1/4 tsp strawberry concentrate, and 1 tbs monkfruit confectioners mix.

Blend and spread over the warm waffle.

Discretionary Cream Cheese Frosting: 1 tbs cream cheddar (room temp), 1/4 tsp strawberry separate, 1 tbs room temp margarine (room temp), and 1 tbs monkfruit confectioners mix.

Combine all fixings and spread over the waffle.

You can likewise top it with basic whipped cream and strawberries.

Custom made whipped cream: 1 cup overwhelming whipping cream, 1 tsp vanilla, 1 tbs monkfruit confectioners mix. Whip until it structures tops. Simple peasy!

Strawberry Shortcake Chaffles. This low carb and keto benevolent Strawberry Shortcake Chaffle is the ideal sweet to appreciate after supper! A sweet chaffle beat with hand crafted keto whipped cream and sweet strawberries! On the off chance that you are searching for a keto strawberry shortcake or a low carb strawberry shortcake then this will before long become your go to!

Strawberry Shortcake Chaffle

Strawberry Shortcake Keto Chaffle Recipe

Strawberry Shortcake Keto Chaffle

This keto Strawberry Shortcake is the most up to date chaffle formula that I am adding to the chaffle plans here on the blog. Furthermore, similar to the next chaffle plans we have shared this one is absolutely delish!

One of my preferred sweets is Strawberry shortcake. I love the sweet kind of the strawberries, blended in with the sweetness of the cake and whipped cream. Anyway my preferred strawberry shortcake formula isn't low carb using any and all means so while adhering to low carb it has been a no go. At that point the keto chaffle formula detonated facebook and I realized I could transform that into a tasty low carb strawberry shortcake formula with a couple tweeks.

I will caution you however, when I was making it I didn't anticipate that it should be as stunning as it turned out. I expected to have a few similitudes, yet not to be great. Anyway the final product is thoroughly astonishing, absolutely great and I presently don't need to leave my strawberry shortcake dessert behind. I would now be able to appreciate it at whatever point I need to!

While this keto chaffle is sufficiently sweet to be a pastry, it is likewise ideal for a high fat low carb breakfast. That is correct, this generally a treat thing can be delighted in for breakfast with no blame by any stretch of the imagination!

What is a Chaffle?

Are every one of your companions discussing chaffles and you are attempting to make sense of what they are? It's alright , they are astonishing and you will cherish them. Be that as it may, just put a chaffle is a waffle made with egg and cheddar. Presently from the essential chaffle formula you can make MANY various assortments of chaffles simply switching up the sort of cheddar that you use.

You can likewise switch up the flavors by adding various things to the fundamental chaffle formula. There are truly unlimited conceivable outcomes when making keto chaffles.

On the off chance that you are new to making chaffles make certain to look at how to make a chaffle for the best keto chaffle formula. This is the place all chaffles, including this pastry chaffle formula start.

Keto Chocolate Chaffle
Blueberry Chaffle
Pizza Chaffle
Cinnamon Roll Chaffle
Chaffle Breakfast Sandwich
Is a Mini Waffle Maker required?

While I like to utilize my dah scaled down waffle producer, you can make this keto strawberry shortcake formula in a huge waffle creator. It will make 3 little chaffles or 1 huge keto chaffle.

Strawberry Shortcake Chaffles Ingredients
Strawberries
granulated swerve
Keto Whipped Cream
Almond flour
egg
mozzarella cheddar
vanilla concentrate

The most effective method to Make Strawberry Shortcake Chaffles

Warmth up your waffle creator. In the event that you are utilizing a smaller than expected waffle producer this formula will make 2 chaffles, if utilizing a huge waffle creator this formula will make 1 huge sweet chaffle.

Wash and hack up your new strawberries. Spot the strawberries in a little bowl and include 1/2 tablespoon granulated swerve. Blend the strawberries in with the swerve and put in a safe spot. In a bowl blend the almond flour, egg, mozzarella cheddar, granulated swerve and vanilla concentrate.

Pour 1/3 of the hitter into your smaller than usual waffle creator and cook for 3-4 minutes. At that point cook another 1/3 of the player and the remainder of the hitter to make 3 keto chaffles.

While your second chaffle is cooking, make your keto whipped cream in the event that you don't have any close by.

Collect your Strawberry Shortcake Chaffle by setting whipped cream and strawberries over your sweet chaffle. At that point shower the juice that will likewise be in the bowl with the strawberries on top.

This formula will make 3 chaffles and you can eat them anyway you decide to. You can stack them and fill the center with whipped cream and top them with strawberries as I did. Or then again you can top every sweet chaffle with whipped cream and strawberries all alone.

CINNAMON ROLL

The best natively constructed cinnamon rolls ever! On the off chance that you love gooey cinnamon buns, here's the mystery fixing. Everybody raves about these natively constructed yeast rolls. You may likewise adore our orange rolls!

Cinnamon rolls are probably the best breakfast. You can make fast and simple cinnamon rolls or you can make cinnamon move hotcakes or bread pudding, yet one of the most delightful approach to serve cinnamon rolls is with this Homemade Cinnamon Roll formula.

Natively constructed Cinnamon Rolls

It's been right around 5 years coming. The young ladies didn't need me to do it, yet we're at last sharing our mystery fixing cinnamon rolls. The without any preparation breakfast sweet rolls that everybody desires. Gooey hand crafted cinnamon rolls. Our best formula that we've been serving loved ones on vacations and some other day for more than 12 years.

We'll get to the mystery fixing, however how about we start directly into how to make these sweet moves, since I realize you would prefer not to burn through whenever. The precise headings and rising occasions are in the formula box underneath, yet here are a few indications for making cinnamon rolls.

How would you make cinnamon rolls?

At the point when I initially set out to make the best cinnamon move formula, I began with this bread mixture. Over that year as I changed the formula, I made the mixture only a slight bit better. The fixings are essential. I like to utilize Red Star Platinum yeast which is a moment yeast. This implies you don't need to let the yeast "verification". On the off chance that you don't utilize moment yeast, make certain to enable the yeast to verification in the warm milk until it is foamy. This will take an additional 5 minutes or somewhere in the vicinity.

Be certain that your milk is warm to initiate the yeast, yet not very hot with the goal that it murders the yeast (around 105-110 degrees Fahrenheit). You'll additionally need to warm the margarine so it is delicate and blends in effectively.

Carry the eggs to room temperature additionally by setting them in a glass of warm water before adding them to the blend. On the off chance that the fixings are not cold, they'll help the yeast to do what it needs to do rapidly and give a wonderful ascent to your cinnamon rolls.

After you have the fixings included, it's a great opportunity to blend the mixture. In the video I utilize a stand blender to blend the mixture. On the off chance that you have bread machine you can utilize the mixture setting to make this amazingly simple. Or on the other hand, go the good old course and get those hands working by plying the bread without a blender. Any way works. In the event that you choose to manipulate with your hands, be mindful so as not to include an excessive amount of flour. The batter should be crude, which is the thing that keeps these custom made cinnamon rolls delicate.

it's imperative to take note of that the mixture will be cheap and delicate. It shouldn't totally stick all over your hands, yet on the off chance that you contact it should feel tasteless and not dry and floury. Try not to be enticed to continue including flour!

After you let the batter ascend in a lubed secured bowl until it is twofold in size, you're good to go the cinnamon rolls. Utilize a cake tangle sprinkled with flour to prevent the mixture from staying.

Keep in mind... the mixture will be shabby and this is where it is alright to include flour the cake tangle and over the batter itself for simple rolling. You'll discover this batter is extremely simple to turn out. In the event that it is a lot of an arm exercise, you've in all probability included an excessive amount of flour.

After you've rolled the mixture, spread the cinnamon topping on top and move off jam move style. Cut into the same number of moves as you'd like. We like to complete 12 moves for a 9×13 skillet (which end up flavorfully enormous!) or in the event that we have to bolster a greater group, 15 moves in a 10×15 preparing container.

Before I had this custom made cinnamon moves formula, I was dependent on Cinnabon cinnamon rolls. They were enormous, delicate, and gooey. I'm about the gooey. I looked and looked (generally formula books since formula sites were not an enormous thing in those days) lastly found a key thought.

Add substantial cream to the cinnamon buns before preparing. THIS is the mystery fixing and what makes the moves rich and gooey. Cinnabon copycat formula? That is not what I was going for, however I think we basically got it.

Here's the manner by which you do it. After the cinnamon folds are folded into their pretty twirls and you've enabled them to ascend in the container... directly before they are prepared to heat, warm overwhelming cream in a little bowl.

Why warm the cream? Since your rolls have ascended in warmth and you would prefer not to add cooler virus cream to your cinnamon rolls. Including warm (not hot!) overwhelming cream will keep the moves ascending as they ought to during heating. Pour the substantial cream overtop the entirety of the rolls and watch that rich cream absorb and around the cinnamon move batter.

This icing contains spread, powdered sugar, cream cheddar and concentrate (either vanilla or maple). You could even toss in a bit of cinnamon to make a cinnamon coat. We've done everything!

You can include the icing while the moves are warm and enable it to absorb, or on the off chance that you'd like an entirely iced look, spread the cream cheddar what tops off an already good thing rolls are at room temperature.

What's more, that my companions, is one of our BEST family plans. My young ladies were reluctant to share our privileged bit of information element for custom made cinnamon rolls, however such huge numbers of you have asked, they hesitantly concurred in light of the fact that they love you and need to see you cheerful.

At the point when you're prepared to heat the moves, prepare and put the moves in the ice chest to defrost medium-term. At that point haul them out of the refrigerate and enable them to rise the morning you need to heat them. Plan about at any rate an hour for this so you aren't standing by excessively long! Enable them to do their subsequent ascent, at that point heat as ordinary.

Mixture Cutter: I JUST got one of these. What have I managed without it every one of these years? Fills in as a scrubber as well, to stall out on batter off surfaces.

Heating Pan 9×13 or 10×15, contingent upon what you need.

Keep in mind... we like to celebrate with GIANT CINNAMON ROLLS!

The best hand crafted cinnamon moves formula with a mystery fixing

Hand crafted Cinnamon Rolls

The best hand crafted cinnamon rolls ever! On the off chance that you love gooey cinnamon buns, here's the mystery fixing. Everybody raves about these custom made yeast rolls.

Course Breakfast

Planning Time 30 minutes

Cook Time 19 minutes

Rise Time 1 hour 10 minutes

Complete Time 1 hour 59 minutes

Servings 12

Calories 618kcal

Creator Julie Clark

Fixings

For the Dough:

1 cup warm milk (around 115 degrees F)

2 1/2 teaspoons moment dry yeast (I like Red Star Platinum Baking Yeast)

2 huge eggs at room temperature

1/3 cup spread softened

4 1/2 cups generally useful flour

1 teaspoon salt

1/2 cup granulated sugar

For the Filling:

1/2 cup spread nearly softened

1 cup stuffed darker sugar

2 tablespoons cinnamon

1/2 cup overwhelming cream (for pouring over the risen rolls)

For the Frosting:

6 ounces cream cheddar (mollified)

1/3 cup spread (relaxed)

2 cups powdered sugar

1/2 tablespoon maple concentrate (or vanilla)

Directions

Pour the warm milk in the bowl of a stand blender and sprinkle the yeast overtop.

Include the eggs, spread, salt and sugar.

Include the flour and blend utilizing the mixer edge just until the fixings are scarcely consolidated. Enable the blend to rest for 5 minutes so the flour has the opportunity to absorb the fluids.

Scratch the batter off the mixer edge and expel it. Join the mixture snare.

Beat the batter on medium speed for 5-7 minutes or until the mixture is flexible and smooth. **The batter will be shabby will at present be adhering to the sides of the bowl. That is alright! Try not to be enticed to include more flour now.

Shower an enormous bowl with cooking splash.

Utilize an elastic spatula to expel the mixture from the blender bowl and spot it in the lubed enormous bowl.

Spread the bowl with a towel or wax paper.

PECAN PIE CHAFFLE

This is a genuine festival from this Southern young lady to you all! I was brought up in the North GA mountains and have affectionate recollections of getting paper sacks brimming with walnuts from my grandparent's back yard. Breaking and shelling them wasn't an excessive amount of fun, yet I realized the prize would be a yummy, gooey, newly prepared walnut pie. I've taken all that flavor and pressed it into a Low Carb Chaffle Cake.

To begin with, I might want to make reference to that this formula is low carb in light of the backstrap molasses fixing. It assists with the shading and the flavor. You can get a lighter, more keto-accommodating formula by including a keto-accommodating syrup in as a trade for this fixing. I would utilize maple syrup from Lakanto or Jordan's thin syrup that has a comparable flavor.

Walnut Pie Filling Ingredients

2 tablespoons spread, mellowed

1 tablespoon Sukrin Gold

1/8 teaspoon blackstrap molasses, discretionary yet assists with shading and flavor

2 tablespoons Maple Bourbon Pecan Skinny Syrup

2 tablespoons overwhelming whipping cream

2 huge egg yolks

Squeeze salt

2 tablespoons walnuts, daintily toasted (I did it in the Airfryer)

Walnut Pie Chaffle Ingredients

1 egg

1 tablespoon overwhelming whipping cream

2 tablespoons cream cheddar, mellowed

1/2 teaspoon maple remove (Olive Nation)

3 tablespoons almond flour

1 tablespoon oat fiber (or another tablespoon almond flour)

1 tablespoon Sukrin Gold

1/2 teaspoon heating powder

2 tablespoons walnuts, slashed

Walnut PIE CHAFFLE CAKE FILLING INSTRUCTIONS

Include margarine, sugar, overwhelming whipping cream and syrups to a little pot on low warmth.

Rush until all around consolidated.

Expel from heat.

Pour 1/2 of the blend into egg yolks and whisk well.

Include that blend once again into the pot while mixing consistently.

Include a touch of salt and walnut.

Let stew until it begins to thicken.

Expel from warmth and let cool while making the Chaffles.

Walnut PIE CHAFFLE CAKE RECIPE INSTRUCTIONS

Blend all fixings aside from walnuts in a little blender for around 15 seconds.

Stop and scratch down the sides with a spatula, and keep blending for an additional 15 seconds until all around mixed.

Blend in walnuts with a spatula.

Pour 3 T of hitter in preheated small waffle creator.

Cook for 1/2 mins.

Expel to cooling rack.

Rehash.

Will make 3 full Chaffles with a modest one for tasting!

Put 1/3 of the walnut pie filling on each Chaffle and gather as wanted!

LEMON MERINGUE CHAFFLE

I am so amped up for this...

This lemon pie possesses a flavor like an eruption of Summertime moving over your tongue!

It takes somewhat longer than the plans that I generally present yet it's going on merit each ounce of exertion that you put into it.

As a matter of first importance, the outside layer is my new most loved low carb pie hull.

It consolidates the fresh sweetness of almond flour with the sandy surface of coconut flour. It's somewhat suggestive of shortbread in the most magnificent manner.

I believe it will need to turn into its very own formula so the entirety of my Keto companions can discover it and fill it with whatever they can consider.

Individuals on the Keto Diet will in general be super (ahem) inventive when searching for low carb dessert options.

Slanting Content from Castle in the Mountains Second, the lemony flavor will make you pucker up (positively).

I was wary about making this pie... lemon pie has consistently been a most loved warm climate treat around here and I was concerned that it would crash and burn against my desires.

In any case, it was fan-cracking tastic and adequate that I needed to share it (not all plans make the cut you know).

Pie Crust

(This post may contain offshoot joins. As an Amazon Associate I will make a little commission at no expense to you when you make a passing buy.)

Tips for a fabulous outside layer:

Ensure your spread is cold.

This is an unquestionable requirement for any pie outside layer, Keto or not. Leave it in the refrigerator until you are prepared to cut it up and hurl it in the nourishment processor.

I really utilize a Ninja blender. I have a nourishment processor yet its enormous and an agony to clean.

The blender accompanies distinctive measured "pitchers" for making an assortment of whatever it is you are making. All aspects of my blender other than the engine is dishwasher safe so... it wins inevitably.

Furthermore, it was extremely reasonable (another success).

Heartbeat the fixings until they are pea measured.

Try not to mix up the outside layer until its "uniform". You need a few bits of margarine in there making your outside flaky and light.

Press the batter into the pie skillet.

I utilized my knuckles and afterward the base of a glass to kind of even it out.

Press in pie coverings are one of my preferred advantages of making Keto pie outside layers... not any more revealing the mixture. It's never been one of my qualities.

Heat the hull and let it cool while you are making the pie filling. It ought to be cool when you finish.

Emptying the filling into a hot pie outside layer will make it spongy and you'll wind up eating your pie with a spoon.

Get together THE FILLING INGREDIENTS....

lemon meringue pie fixings

It will be simpler on the off chance that you separate your eggs into yolks and whites and beat the yolks in a grain bowl or something comparative.

You'll require space to "temper" the eggs with the hot blend later all the while.

You'll be utilizing both egg whites and yolks in the event that you intend to make the meringue.

Lemon pizzazz is significant and it develops the kind of the filling.

The formula records 2-3 tablespoons of pizzazz. I zested every one of the four lemons and utilized anyway a lot of I had on the grounds that I love the harshness that it includes.

It's a "to taste" kind of fixing.

Ground cardamom is discretionary.

Yet, you should utilize it on the off chance that you have it. I can't depict the flavor aside from citrusy, and home grown.

Cardamom fabricates the pie's flavor in intricacy and whoever is sufficiently fortunate to impart it to you will be left thinking about what the mystery fixing is.

What to do in the event that you don't have psyllium husk powder...

Purchase some...just joking.

—

In any case, not so much, get some for some time later on the grounds that it destroys thickener.

I like psyllium husk powder due to the fiber and the surface. Be that as it may, I know not every person keeps it close by. Also, it's not in every case promptly accessible at a market (yet).

You can utilize 2 teaspoons of arrowroot powder if important. (Even my supermarket in the sticks has it).

I truly cant address how much thickener to utilize on the grounds that I don't utilize it any longer. I wager it would work... I simply cant help with the conversion scale.

Since I found how much simpler psyllium husk powder functions, tastes and the stunning medical advantages it has... I have been utilizing it only in my prepared products starting late. On the off chance that YOU WILL BE MAKING THE MERINGUE...

I truly like my Lemon Pie with whipped cream.

I have never been a tremendous devotee of meringue yet individuals like it. It keeps well in the cooler and ventures well (Whipped cream DOES NOT).

What's more, it looks excellent so I remembered meringue for this formula and even put it on BOTH of my Lemon Pies.

For what reason did I make two pies?

Since I "over beat" the meringue on the principal pie.

I beat the egg whites until they were frothy like a bowl loaded with dish washing fluid.

This is the thing that occurred....

over beaten meringue

Do you see that emptied out arch of crunchy meringue like stuff?

That's right. It looked delightful outwardly however I was really frustrated with the last item.

Despite everything we ate it... however a crunchy and super-sweet garnish was not what I was going for.

It was alright in light of the fact that it was then that I understood it required more thickener... and I had the option to caution you about over beating the eggs.

(I have never had this occur and at first accused the erythritol lol.)

Side note:

Since I made two pies and attempted two pies and LOVE lemon pie, I went WAY over my cutoff of erythritol... and it was revolting.

While I won't (over)share precisely what occurred, I will let you know this..only eat each cut in turn.

Try not to OVERDO IT regardless of the amount you love lemon pie.

This formula calls for hardened tops for the meringue... not froth.

It should look something like this.

hardened crested meringue

Simply thud the egg whites over the filling and spread to the outside.

There is no smooth method to do this. On the off chance that you have never made meringue, don't stress.

You'll get the hang of spreading it out before long.

Which is great since you would prefer not to delay a lot now. Try not to let the meringue flatten a lot before you seal it up and get this infant in the broiler.

meringue on pie

Ensure the meringue seals the whole pie in.

I don't have a clue why you must be cautious about this, I simply realize you do.

My Gram resembled Wonder Woman in the kitchen and she repeated this point so a lot of that I have never attempted to make sense of what occurs on the off chance that you don't close it... .

Perhaps it spills out? Possibly it flattens? I don't have the foggiest idea yet you should simply pursue her recommendation and be cautious with this progression.

The pinnacles of the meringue ought to be a light brilliant dark colored.

Since the pie outside is fixed in you would truly need to prepare it for quite a while to consume it..but consumed meringue isn't great either.

Prepare for 30-35 minutes or until sautéed and it doesn't shake when you squirm the pie skillet.

THAT'S IT...

I trust you make the most of your lemon pie and please let me know in the remarks underneath in the event that you have any inquiries or very marvelous increases!

KETO LEMON MERIGUE PIE

I LOVE LEMON PIE! It's invigorating and just poses a flavor like Summer. This is an incredible formula for an uncommon event or after a flavorful dinner. You can make this with or without the meringue. I would state this low carb treat takes a smidgen of kitchen abilities however anybody can pull it off in the event that you adhere to the directions.

Print Pin Rate

Course: DessertCuisine: American, keto dessert, low carb dessertKeyword: keto dessert, keto lemon merigue pie, Low carb lemon merigue pie Prep Time: 30 minutesCook Time: 30 minutesCooling Time: 5 hoursTotal Time: 1 hour Servings: 8 Slices Calories: 294kcal Author: Brenna Ring

Fixings

Pie Crust

1/2 Cup Almond Flour

1/2 Cup Coconut Flour

2 Tbsp Erythritol

2 tsp Psyllium Husk powder

2 huge eggs

1/2 cup Butter (salted) cubed and VERY cold

Pie Filling

1 Cup Erythritol

1 bundle Unflavored Gelatin I utilized Knox

4 Egg Yolks beaten (save whites for meringue)

1 Cup Water

1 tbsp Psyllium Husk Powder

3 tbsp Salted Cream Butter

1 Cup Lemon Juice Fresh is ideal. I utilized four lemons.

2-3 tbsp Lemon Zest I zested each of the four lemons and utilized what I had. This is a "to taste" sort of fixing.

1 tsp ground cardamom discretionary

* Meringue

4 Egg Whites

1/2 tsp Cream of Tartar

1/8-1/4 cup low carb sugar *to taste (see notes in post)

US Customary - Metric

Get Ingredients Powered by Chicory

Guidelines

Pie Crust
Preheat broiler to 350F
Put everything into a blender or nourishment processor and heartbeat until it the consistency of pieces.
Press into a pie plate and heat for 10-12 minutes.
Significant: Let the outside layer cool totally before you fill it.
Pie Crust
Filling
Beat the egg yolks in a bowl and let sit until the subsequent stage is finished.
Join sugar, gelatin, psyllium husk powder, and water in a pan. Heat to the point of boiling for one moment while always mixing with a whisk.
Empty a portion of the blend into the bowl with the beaten eggs while mixing (this is called treating).
Empty the egg blend again into the pot and stew until thickened. Try not to allow this to bubble! IT HAS TO THICKEN IN THE PAN OR IT WILL STAY SOUPY. Prop stirring....it's up to look somewhat vile and unusual from the outset. This will level out in the following stage.
Race in the salted spread, lemon juice and lemon get-up-and-go. Expel from warmth and let cool for 20 minutes.
Immerse your pie covering and let cool to room temp or put it in the ice chest to speed it up.
In the event that you are including the meringue, move onto the subsequent stage.
On the off chance that you will be beating your pie with whipped cream, leave the pie in the ice chest until cold and you are prepared to serve.
Merigue
Let the pie filling cool for in any event 15 minutes at room temp or put it in the cooler for 10 minutes to speed this up.
* This is significant. It would be ideal if you see tips in the post.
Whip the egg whites, cream of tartar and sugar until hardened pinnacles frame yet don't over beat. *see tips in post
I utilize a Kitchen help for this progression however

—

A CHAFFLE BY ANY OTHER NAME

TACO CHAFFLES

This Crispy Taco Chaffle Recipe is completely mouth-watering flavorful! It was such an unbelievable expansion to the Very Best Taco Meat, and the firm taco shells were superior to anything I envisioned.

Taco Chaffle Recipe: Crispy, Not Eggy, and Delicious!

Taco servings of mixed greens are one of our preferred simple family dinners. Every one of the four children love tacos. They can make the most of theirs on tortillas, while the centers and I eat taco plates of mixed greens or here and there keto taco cups. I've taken a stab at making taco dishes simply out of cheddar, and despite the fact that I love the crunch, they are constantly somewhat oily.

At that point, enter all the Keto Chaffle absurdity that has set the keto world ablaze of late. As I was preparing supper the previous evening, I realized that I could make a Chaffle Taco Shell effectively. While there are numerous chaffle plans on the web, I realized that this one should have been incredibly firm and not eggy at all or it could never go as a taco shell.

My most established girl and I began testing and thought of without a doubt the ideal and firm taco shell chaffle. It was so great; I needed to make more since we adored it to such an extent. I've incorporated all the data you need underneath on the off chance that you aren't exactly cutting-edge on this chaffle insane.

Anyway, What in the World is a Chaffle?

I know. It has been a serious week in the keto network. On the off chance that you took some time off or haven't invested any energy in Facebook gatherings, you may have passed up the chaffle rage. A Chaffle is a waffle made on a Dash Mini Waffle Maker with eggs and cheddar. Since that formula turned out, there have been incalculable varieties posted, and some don't have any cheddar as a fixing. This formula for Keto Taco Chaffles is a variety of the first formula that I tried until I got an ideal firm taco shell chaffle. Make a point to look at this rundown of Ultimate Tips for Best Keto Chaffle Recipes.

What Do I Use to Make a Keto Taco Chaffle?

The Dash Mini Waffle Maker is the one kitchen machine that the keto world has been set for find. This smaller than usual waffle producer makes one four-inch waffle. While you could utilize a normal waffle producer, there is something in particular about this smaller than expected one that gets Chaffles pleasant and firm. Maybe it is on the grounds that the meshes are littler and closer together or the way that it gets so hot, however in any case, there is no uncertainty that on the off chance that you pursue the Keto Diet, you are going to see many plans for this item.

For the individuals who may feel that creation each chaffle in turn is excessively particular, this waffle creator is an extraordinary alternative. It makes four 3 inch waffles without a moment's delay. Since it makes littler Chaffles, you'd have to utilize somewhat less hitter, however it could be a tremendous timesaver on the off chance that you are making a few Keto Chaffle taco shells on the double.

Where Can I Find the Dash Mini Waffle Maker?

On the off chance that you would prefer not to go around town on a scrounger chase searching for a waffle creator in stores, you can put in a request on Amazon. The way that Amazon conveys without me hauling every one of my children around town implies that it is forever my first decision. In the event that you need to get one without requesting check Bed Bath and Beyond, TJ Maxx, Kohl's, Walmart, or Target.

To begin with, I began by tossing every one of the fixings in a little bowl. I utilized a blend of thicker destroyed cheddar for Taco Chaffles.

Daintily oil the Dash Mini Waffle Maker. At that point, I spooned out portion of the chaffle player onto the waffle iron. This chaffle taco formula makes two chaffles. You can without much of a stretch twofold or triple the formula to make more at once.

Keto Chaffle in the scramble smaller than usual waffle creator cooked

When you pour the hitter on the waffle creator, close the top and don't contact for 4 minutes. I attempted to check mine part of the way through cooking and nearly discarded it as it looked as though it wasn't going to set up appropriately. It needs the full four minutes to get a decent brilliant dark colored shading and to fresh appropriately.

When the Taco Chaffle shells were done, I turned over a biscuit container and collapsed them fifty-fifty between two tins. As they cooled, they remained looking like a taco shell.

Are these Chaffle Taco Shells Crispy?

Truly! They are overly firm. They aren't eggy at all either. This Taco Chaffle formula makes incredibly crunchy taco shells that aren't oily by any stretch of the imagination.

For the flavorful ground hamburger taco meat, I recommend utilizing my most established girl's formula for the Very Best Taco Meat with my custom made keto-accommodating taco flavoring. This formula is the best taco meat I've at any point eaten. It has so a lot of mind blowing striking flavor. I in every case twofold the formula so we can appreciate it for lunch for a few days or freeze for some other time. On the off chance that you lean toward chicken, this slow cooker formula for Low Carb Mexican Shredded Chicken would be phenomenal also.

Blessed smokes, the Taco Chaffle Recipe was delectable!! It made an ideal low carb firm taco shell that we've all been absent.

Garnishes for Taco Chaffles

There are such huge numbers of keto low carb well-disposed choices for fixing Keto Taco Chaffles. I've incorporated those I could consider beneath:

harsh cream
guacamole
lettuce
destroyed cheddar
diced onions
diced tomatoes
jalapeños
Taco Chaffle formula with ground hamburger, lettuce, and cheddar

Would i be able to Make This Easy Keto Recipe Ahead of Time? You could unquestionably make the Keto Chaffle Taco Shells early just as the taco meat. In any case, I would recommend not rewarming the taco shells in the microwave as they would lose their freshness. Rather, I envelop by aluminum foil and rewarm in the broiler or pop them noticeable all around fryer.

More Keto Chaffle Recipes:

Exceptionally Popular Traditional Keto Chaffle Recipe

Chocolate Chip Chaffle Keto Recipe

Pizza Chaffle Keto Recipe

Keto Pumpkin Keto Waffle Recipe (Chaffle)

Blueberry Keto Chaffle

Keto Chaffle Breakfast Sandwich with almond flour

Scaled down Keto Pizza with Chaffle Pizza Crust (almond flour)

Strawberry Shortcake Chaffle Recipe

Keto Chaffle Taco Shells Recipe with almond flour

WASABI CHAFFLES

LOADED CHAFFLES NACHOS

Fixings

2 eggs

1 cup mozzarella

1/2 cheddar (I included this, you can include another cheddar)

2 TBSP Almond flour

1 tsp garlic

1 jalepeno diced

2 strips bacon

Garnishes (pick one or all)

Taco meat

Harsh cream

Guacamole

Olives

Salsa

Jalapeno cuts

Onions

Steps

Blended fixings, at that point cook in waffle producer. At the point when concocted tear or use kitchen scissors to cut up.

Layer dish with chaffles, mozzarella, cheddar, more jalapenos and taco meat. I included sweet banana peppers too.

Cook in 425 degree stove for 10 minutes or more on the off chance that you need a crisper base.

Notes

Nourishment Facts (garnishes excluded, change your macros dependent on fixings you include)

Servings: 4

Sum per 1 serving

Calories   202

Absolute Fat 15.6g

Absolute Carbohydrate 2.7g

Dietary Fiber 0.8g

Absolute Sugars 0.5g

Protein 13.4g

MOZZARELLA PANINI

Fixings

4 crusty bread sandwich rolls

2 tablespoons olive oil

1/2 cup basil pesto

8 cuts mozzarella cheddar

1 medium tomato, cut into 8 slim cuts

1/2 teaspoon salt

1/4 teaspoon pepper

Steps

1 Warmth shut contact flame broil 5 minutes.

2 Cut each move down the middle on a level plane; brush outside of every half with oil. Spread pesto on within the two parts. Layer each sandwich with cheddar and tomato. Sprinkle with salt and pepper.

3 At the point when barbecue is warmed, place sandwiches on flame broil. Close flame broil; barbecue 4 minutes or until bread is toasty and cheddar is dissolved. Cut sandwiches on corner to corner and serve warm.

Master Tips

On the off chance that you can't discover crusty bread moves, you can substitute focaccia or 8 cuts of nation bread.

This sandwich is particularly scrumptious when made with huge beefsteak tomatoes at their pinnacle of readiness. At the point when ready tomatoes are not accessible, take a stab at utilizing cleaved cherry tomatoes. They are all the more dependably delightful regardless of what the season.

New mozzarella can be utilized rather than the cuts.

PIZZA CHAFFLE

Fixings

FOR PIZZA CHAFFLES:

2 huge eggs

2 tbsp. almond flour

1/2 tsp. legitimate salt

1/2 tsp. preparing pop

1/2 c. destroyed mozzarella, separated

1/3 c. pepperoni cuts

Newly ground Parmesan, for serving

Bearings

Preheat waffle creator as per maker's headings. In a medium bowl, whisk eggs, almond flour, salt, and preparing soft drink together. Include 1 cup mozzarella and mix to cover.

Pour 1/2 cup blend into focal point of waffle creator and cook until brilliant and fresh, 2 to 3 minutes. Rehash with residual hitter.

Promptly top with marinara, remaining ½ cup mozzarella, pepperoni, and a sprinkle of Parmesan.

CONCLUSION

I hope you enjoyed your journey through this **Keto Chaffle Recipes**. It is essential to adhere to the contexts of this book to achieve that very best weight you have ever thought of. Happy Reading.

CPSIA information can be obtained
at www.ICGtesting.com
Printed in the USA
BVHW041755190421
605313BV00011B/291

9 781801 604192